5-MINUTE
BIBLE STUDIES

for

FAMILIES

Jay Bickelhaupt

NORTHWESTERN PUBLISHING HOUSE
Milwaukee, Wisconsin

Northwestern Publishing House
N16W23379 Stone Ridge Dr., Waukesha, WI 53188-1109
www.nph.net
© 2020 Northwestern Publishing House
Published 2020
Printed in the United States of America
ISBN 978-0-8100-3020-6
ISBN 978-0-8100-3021-3 (e-book)

21 22 23 24 25 26 27 28 29   10 9 8 7 6 5 4 3 2

Getting to Know God

The Only Connection

❖

Amy never sat on Grandpa's lap because he lived thousands of miles away. Yet she knew that Grandpa was bald with a long handlebar mustache and that he loved to tell silly jokes. She knew her Grandpa because she would connect with him through the internet at least once every week. What is even more important than connecting with family and having friends is connecting with God and getting to know him. So, how do you get to know and stay connected to God?

**Jesus answered, "I am the way and the truth and the life.
No one comes to the Father except through me.
If you really know me, you will know my Father as well.
From now on, you do know him and have seen him."** JOHN 14:6,7

Technology allows us to see, hear, and get to know others. However, God doesn't have an email address or a smart phone so that we can connect with him. Your connection with God was actually cut off because of your sin. But long before the internet, smart phones, and social media arrived on the scene, there was Jesus. Jesus is what connects you to God because Jesus is the one who forgives your sins. Jesus is your Savior who lets you know what God is like and what God has done to give you eternal life. If you believe in Jesus, you know God **as** Father; but what's even more awesome, the Father knows you!

- Identify the special relationship God has with you and you have with God.

- Name three things you can do to to keep connected to the Father.

Thank Jesus for connecting you to the true God and for the relationship you have with him.

Getting to Know God

How God Loves Me

❖

Take 15 seconds and think about one way you can show love.
There are many ways and things people do to show love. But how does God love you?

For God so loved the world that he gave his one and only Son, that whoever believes in him shall not perish but have eternal life. JOHN 3:16

There may be days when you wonder if God could love you. You feel terrible over the nasty words you said, the hurtful things you did, or the ways you failed to love your friend. You think, "How could God love a sinner like me?" But if you look, you will see the many ways that God loves you. He gives you food and clothes. He created green grass, blue skies, and twinkling stars for you to enjoy. But your shirt doesn't cover up your sin. The sky doesn't block your failures from God as he looks down from heaven. Yet God decided to show love by giving you his only Son! Jesus was sent from heaven so that he could give himself on the cross to be punished for all your failures—all your nasty words and actions—so that you will never be punished. God loved the world and because you have Jesus in your life, you have God's amazing love!

- List the fears that God's love removes from your life.

- Fill in how you would finish this sentence: "I show God's

  love to my family when I _____."

Pray that the Holy Spirit fills your heart with the joy of Jesus' forgiveness, salvation, and perfect love.

Getting to Know God

Always Predictable

❖

Do you like change? Think of two things that change every day that you like and two things that change that you don't like.
Christians can be thankful that God doesn't change.

I the LORD do not change. MALACHI 3:6

The weather can change, which causes some to put away their shorts and pull out their long underwear. The school lunch menu changes, which can cause some to pack a lunch. Some changes are good. It can be fun to try different ice cream and discover your new favorite flavor. It can be fun to take a trip and see how the country changes as you travel through the plains and over mountains and on to the ocean. Things change all around you. That can be scary. At the same time, change can be exciting. But what if God changed like the weather, so that you didn't know whether to expect an angry God who thundered at you or a loving God who would warmly smile upon you? When you worry, you are really thinking that God can change. You know his promises, his love, and that he forgives you; but worry shows that you think God can break his promise and change his attitude about you, or forget about you. The Lord doesn't change! Thankfully, Jesus is always quick to forgive our sin of worry. Jesus can never break his promises to you and will never stop loving you—because he doesn't change.

- List at least four promises God gives to you that you know will never change.

- For each listed promise, tell how that promise chases away your worries.

Ask your God, who can't change, to help you with the changes that you don't like, which are happening in your lives.

3

King of Creation

No Guessing

❖

Name one of the first things a teacher asks students to do when they are making a project or filling out a worksheet: Put your name on it! The teacher doesn't want to take the time to figure out whose project it is. If there is no name on the paper, then you won't receive the grade you deserve.

Who gets credit for making everything that you can see, feel, touch, taste, and hear? Who gets the credit for making you?

In the beginning God created the heavens and the earth.
GENESIS 1:1

What do you need when you build something? You need materials like building blocks, clay, paper, glue, or wood. It would be impossible for you to build something out of the air, out of nothing. But building something out of nothing wasn't impossible for God. In the beginning there was no air to breathe. There was no dirt to mound up. There was no tape to hold things together. There was nothing except God and his powerful Word who created what you see above and what you enjoy on earth below. In the Bible God signs his name to his creation so that he gets the credit for what he has made; and everything he made was good. You don't have to guess who made the stars that twinkle millions of miles away or where the world came from. You know the Creator and the Creator knows you!

- What can you learn about God by knowing that he made everything out of nothing?

- List things God created that give you the following reactions.
  - Happy—
  - Excited—
  - Curious—
  - Amazed—

Praise your Creator for some of the things that you were able to enjoy today.

King of Creation

No One Is Faster Than God

❖

It takes time to do whatever we do, whether we are cleaning, playing, going to school, or even sleeping. It took time for God to create the world. Do you know how long it took?

In six days the LORD made the heavens and the earth, the sea, and all that is in them, but he rested on the seventh day. EXODUS 20:11

Some museum plaques read, "Billions of years ago the world came into being because of the Big Bang." The Bible doesn't speak of a Big Bang creating the world, but that the Lord made everything. God made the creepy crawlies that give us the willies, and he made the sea creatures that are as big as a bus. God made all things perfectly, and he did it all in only six days!

If you run really fast in a race, you might get a first place ribbon for being the best. You can't pin a first place ribbon on the Lord's chest for making the universe quickly, but you can praise him for his almighty power, and for his creativity as he made so many interesting animals, places, and things. In six days your Lord created it all, and on the seventh day he stopped creating. God has given you a seven-day week in which to worship him and enjoy all that he has made.

- What is one of your favorite places to visit? What about that place shows God's amazing power?

- What did God create on each day? If you have a piece of paper, draw a picture of what he made on each day.

Thank the Lord for the time that he gives you in life to enjoy all that he has made.

King of Creation

We Are God's People

❖

Mrs. Frank was delighted to see the beautiful picture of a sunset that hung in her classroom. The reds and oranges were so bright that she felt as if her face could feel the warmth of the sun. Yet, she felt sad because she had no idea to whom it belonged. Mrs. Frank knew that it belonged to someone because someone had to have made it.

To whom do you belong?

Know that the LORD is God. It is he who made us, and we are his; we are his people, the sheep of his pasture. PSALM 100:3

There are probably things that you don't want to take credit for. You might not want to take responsibility for the mess that you made, because then you would have to clean it up. God doesn't try to hide the fact that he made you, even though you make your life messy by the unkind things you say and the unloving actions you do. God announces to the world that he made you and he then washes away your sin through the blood of Jesus. God wants you to be close to him as sheep are kept close to their shepherd who cares for them and watches over them. Belonging to a family makes you feel loved. Belonging to the Lord promises that you will be loved forever!

- What can you do to show others that you belong to God?

- How are you going to thank God for the talents he gave you?

Pray that the Lord would continue to lead your family and protect you as his sheep.

Skilled Sculptor

Take Your Time

❖

When doing a project at home or school, have you ever been told to take your time or to stay in the lines when you are coloring? Don't get glue all over the place. Why are you told these things?
God is a skilled sculptor who took his time making the first man.

The LORD God formed a man from the dust of the ground and breathed into his nostrils the breath of life, and the man became a living being. GENESIS 2:7

The Lord didn't go to the local craft store to get the materials he needed to make his special project. God used what he already had made on day number three. And God didn't say, "Let there be," when it came to man and woman. He took his time to show that human beings are a very special part of his creation. Out of the dust of the ground the Lord formed person—like a skilled sculptor who works clay with his fingers. Imagine God taking his time to form the man's nose, fingers, and legs just perfectly. Now imagine the pile of dust shaped into a person. The dust was lifeless and couldn't move, that is, until God breathed into his nostrils the breath of life. In an instant, the man's lungs started to breathe, his heart started to beat, and his body became living and active. God took his time when he made people, and what he made was very good.

- What do you think it was like when God breathed into the dust he formed and Adam came to life?

- List at least five things about the human body that show God's wisdom and love.

Pray that God keeps you and your loved ones safe from all harm and danger.

Skilled Sculptor

God's Image

❖

What was the most incredible thing that God created? Think about the millions of stars, the galaxies, the oceans filled with wild creatures, and the snowcapped mountains. What is at the top of God's list of the most incredible things he made?

Then God said, "Let us make mankind in our image, in our likeness, so that they may rule over the fish in the sea and the birds in the sky, over the livestock and all the wild animals, and over all the creatures that move along the ground." So God created mankind in his own image, in the image of God he created them; male and female he created them. GENESIS 1:26,27

God did something when he made man that he didn't do with any other part of his creation. The Father, the Son, and the Holy Spirit had a conversation and decided to make man in their image and likeness. Human beings aren't just animals in the animal kingdom. God created humans in his image and gave each person a soul. That doesn't mean Adam looked like God physically, but it does mean that Adam was like God spiritually. Adam and Eve had no sin and wanted to do what God wanted them to do. God created many mind-blowing things, but the greatest part of creation is that he made Adam and Eve in his image and gave them his creation to rule over.

- What makes a person different from the rest of the living creatures?

- God created Adam and Eve to rule over his creation. What has God given you to rule over and how does he want you to rule?

Thank God for creating the people who love and care for you.

Skilled Sculptor

God Knows Me

❖

How does it make you feel when people don't care about you? Maybe someone has forgotten your birthday, your name, or didn't include you in a game. It hurts! But God doesn't forget about you and he doesn't stop caring for you.

You created my inmost being; you knit me together in my mother's womb. All the days ordained for me were written in your book before one of them came to be. PSALM 139:13,16

Before you were born, God already knew you. God knows about every single day you will live, breathe, play, learn, and serve the Lord on earth before they even happen. God cares for you so much that he carefully knit you together as a unique person with special gifts, talents, physical features, and personality. God gave you emotions that allow you to be sad, happy, and silly. God gave you a mind to think about and to know Jesus as your Savior. The Holy Spirit gave you faith so you can trust that the Lord will never forget you; there is not one day in your entire life that he will fail to care for you. God knew you from eternity, and he will know you throughout eternity!

- Sometimes it does hurt and makes us feel lonely when someone forgets about us. How does it make you feel knowing that the Lord knew you before you even were born and promises that he knows every single day you will live on earth?

- God made each person unique. Name one special thing that you enjoy about a friend or family member.

Praise God for making you and for always remembering you.

Horrible, No Good Sin

The Worst Day Ever!

❖

Have you ever had the worst day ever? What made the day so bad? We might be able to look back (or sometimes we might not want to look back) on the very bad, no good day that we personally experienced. But is there a day that could be considered the worst day ever experienced in the history of the world? There is!

**The LORD God commanded the man,
"You must not eat from the tree of the knowledge of good
and evil, for when you eat from it you will certainly die."
When the woman saw that the fruit of the tree was good
for food and pleasing to the eye, and also desirable
for gaining wisdom, she took some and ate it.
She also gave some to her husband, who was with her,
and he ate it.** GENESIS 2:16,17; 3:6

Everything God made was good and perfect! Adam and Eve lived in the Garden of Eden. At first they showed God that they loved and trusted in him by not eating fruit from the tree of the knowledge of good and evil, but Eve listened to the devil's lies and was tempted to eat the forbidden fruit. She disobeyed God and gave some fruit to Adam who ate too. They did not drop dead, but spiritually they died and were no longer good, but rather, sinful. Oh, it was the worst day in history when sin entered the world! How blest we are, that God promised to fix the worst day ever by sending Jesus!

- God made everything good! Is he to blame for sin being in the world? How blest we are, that God promised to fix the worst day ever by sending Jesus! Who is responsible for sin?

- How does it feel to be called a sinner? What do we know we need because we are sinful?

Ask God to forgive all your sins because of Jesus, who lived and died for you.

Horrible, No Good Sin

God's Target

❖

Charlie ran for cover when he became everyone's target during the snow-ball fight. Would you like to be the target of a snowball fight? It might depend on who is throwing the snowballs. How would you feel if God made you his target?

> **Like the rest, we were by nature deserving of wrath.
> But because of his great love for us, God, who is rich
> in mercy, made us alive with Christ
> even when we were dead in transgressions—
> it is by grace you have been saved.** EPHESIANS 2:3-5

God hates sin. Because we are born with sin, we deserve God's punishment and anger. We deserve to be God's targets of wrath! There is no place to which we can run and hide from our all-knowing God. He is everywhere all of the time. What will we do? The good news is that we don't have to do anything to earn God's favor. We can't do anything to save ourselves or wash our sins away. One of the greatest words in the Bible is *but.* "We were by nature deserving of wrath. *But* because of his great love for us." God came to our rescue because he made us the target, not of his anger, but of his love. God doesn't give us the punishment we deserve, instead he gave our punishment to Jesus on the cross to save us. We are saved because God made us the target of his grace.

- God saved you when you were dead in transgressions (sins). What does this tell you about how much you can help with your salvation?

- What can you expect in life if you are a target of Jesus' grace?

Thank God for giving you forgiveness and salvation in Jesus.

Horrible, No Good Sin

The Toughest Wrestling Match

❖

Have you ever wrestled? There are different ways to wrestle. You may have the title of king or queen of the living room floor. Or maybe you like to challenge your brain by wrestling with math problems or difficult puzzles. What about the spiritual wrestling matches you find yourself in every day? How do you win those?

I know that good itself does not dwell in me, that is, in my sinful nature. For I do not do the good I want to do, but the evil I do not want to do—this I keep on doing. What a wretched man I am! Who will rescue me from this body that is subject to death? Thanks be to God, who delivers me through Jesus Christ our Lord!
ROMANS 7:18,19,24,25

Sinners want to sin. Have you ever found yourself wanting to do good things but ended up hurting a friend or even family members with your words? Because of our sinful natures, we can't do the good things we want to do. The apostle Paul screams, "What a wretched man I am!" Who is going to rescue us from our sin and from death? Jesus Christ our Lord will and has. Jesus did not have a sinful nature, but he still wrestled with temptation. And he won. Jesus is the undisputed champion over sin! Jesus never sinned so that he could rescue you from your sinful nature and give you eternal life.

- God tells you that you are going to wrestle with your sinful nature all your life. What does that mean you need every day?

- How can you show your thankfulness for Jesus?

Ask God to give you strength to say no to temptation.

12

One for All

The First Promise

❖

The only command that Adam and Eve had was not to eat from the tree of the knowledge of good and evil. Or you know what happened. Eve ate some fruit and gave some to Adam, who ate it too. God's promise came true. If they ate of the fruit, they would die—and spiritually they did. But God went to them, and they heard the first promise of a Savior.

**I will put enmity between you and the woman,
and between your offspring and hers;
he will crush your head, and you will strike his heel.**
GENESIS 3:15

Have you been told that it isn't nice to hate? To understand the promise God gave to Adam and Eve, remember that Eve befriended the devil by listening to his lies. Sinners would continue to listen to the devil if it were not for God's grace and power. God causes your heart to hate that which is evil and sinful. Praise God for that! You don't want Satan's lies because you have the truth! God promised that the Savior would be born of a woman and that he would come to crush the devil's head. If your head gets crushed, what does that mean for your body? It is useless and powerless. Jesus crushed Satan's power and he no longer controls you. Jesus loves you so much that he would suffer on the cross to save you from sin and death. One man fell into sin, and one Savior was promised in order to rescue you from the curse of sin.

- What do you think it means that the devil would strike Jesus' heel?

- Why is this passage often read during the season of Advent?

Praise God for giving the promise of a Savior and fulfilling the promise in Jesus.

One for All

Not Just an Example

❖

Some people think Jesus came to earth to be an example for us to follow in order to get to heaven. They are seriously mistaken. Jesus came as the Savior who would rescue from sin and give the perfection that is needed. Jesus is more than your example—he is your Savior.

**Then Jesus was led by the Spirit into the wilderness
to be tempted by the devil. Jesus said to him,
"Away from me, Satan! For it is written:
'Worship the Lord your God, and serve him only.'"
Then the devil left him, and angels came and attended him.**
MATTHEW 4:1,10,11

Jesus was tempted just like you are, but he never sinned. You are tempted like Jesus was, but you have sinned. It is hard not to worry. There are scary things in the world, so sometimes you do worry. That is sin! Have you ever been jealous of the toys, craft supplies, and the cool things that your friends have? Jealousy is sin! You aren't perfect! That is why Jesus was perfect for you. He didn't worship Satan to get more stuff. He didn't worry that he was going to die in the desert. God demands that you be perfect in every way, so he gave you a perfect Savior who lived a perfect life for you. You are holy not because you follow Jesus' example. You are holy because Jesus never gave into temptation and never sinned!

- What did Jesus use to drive Satan far from him? Why is that so comforting for you?

- You wear Jesus' holiness through faith in him. Who does God the Father see when he looks at you?

Thank Jesus for his robe of righteousness that you wear.

One for All

It Took Just One

❖

Have you ever gotten in trouble for something someone else did? It doesn't feel good to be punished when you didn't do anything wrong.. You didn't commit the first sin in the Garden of Eden, but it took just one sin for you to be sinful.

If, by the trespass of the one man, death reigned through that one man, how much more will those who receive God's abundant provision of grace and of the gift of righteousness reign in life through the one man, Jesus Christ! ROMANS 5:17

There was one command, one Eve, one Adam, and one act of disobedience against one Holy God. Sin ruined God's creation. The animals he created now die. Cemeteries are filled because people die. Sin is in the world and death is the ugly king that reigns. There is nothing that people can do about it! That is why God had to do everything about it. Did you notice who reigns because of Jesus Christ? You do! You have received God's promise of love and forgiveness through your baptism. When you read or hear the Word, God promises that you have a perfect relationship with him because of Jesus. Jesus is your risen Savior who rules *for* you and *in* you! It took just one Savior, who lived and died for you, to save you from sin and death. Not only will you live in heaven with Jesus, but you will rule forever with him too!

- Why don't you have to be afraid of death?

- What does it mean that you have received the gift of righteousness?

Thank God the Father that you have a right relationship with him through Jesus.

Giving From What Is Given

A Giver's Heart

❖

What was one of the best gifts you have ever received? What made that gift so special? As God's people, we have the privilege to give gifts to the Lord that please him. What makes our gifts so special to the Lord?

**Abel also brought an offering—fat portions
from some of the firstborn of his flock.
The LORD looked with favor on Abel
and his offering.** GENESIS 4:4

Not many people were living on earth at this time in history. We aren't told about any church buildings, and the Bible doesn't even mention an altar in the lesson. Yet Abel offered some of his flock to the Lord. Abel believed the promise of the coming Savior from sin, which he heard from his parents who heard the promise themselves in the Garden of Eden. Faith filled Abel's heart, and even though we don't know about a command to bring offerings, Abel willingly brought some of the gifts God had first given to him. Gifts that are given from hearts of faith please God. Abel didn't give the lame or sick sheep to the Lord. From a heart of faith Abel gave God the firstborn, the best, and the fattest ones. Why would Abel do such a thing? It was because God promised to give Abel, and all of us, his best when he sent Jesus to be our Savior.

- What can we learn from Abel when it comes to giving God our best?

- What attitudes are pleasing to God when it comes to giving an offering?

Pray that the Lord blesses his people with generous and joyful hearts when they plan their offerings.

Giving From What Is Given

My Stuff

❖

How much stuff do you have? Do you have a pillow, shoes, a backpack, and at least one toy? Would all of your stuff fill up a grocery bag? Would your stuff fill a wheelbarrow or maybe even a dump truck? You might have very little or you might have very much, but where did all of your stuff come from?

**Everything comes from you [the Lord],
and we have given you only what comes from your hand.**
1 CHRONICLES 29:14

King David was amazed at how much God's people gave for building a temple to the Lord. They gave dump truck loads of gold and silver. There were piles of twinkling precious stones also offered to the Lord. Try to imagine the incredible wealth! You probably could have gone sledding down the hills of gold and all of the stuff that the Israelites gave. But did you notice that they didn't give *to* the Lord? They gave *from* what God had given to them. King David praises God as the one who makes all things and really owns all things. God's people gave very generously because they understood that everything they had was God's stuff. The stuff in your house, desk, locker, garage, or backyard really isn't your stuff to keep forever. Everything you have comes from God, including your most precious treasure— the forgiveness of sins. And everything you give, you give *from* him.

- Everything you have is on loan from God. How does that move you to use and treat the things you have?

- Does your family have a plan to give generously to the Lord? Talk about the plan you have or about making a plan to give from what God has given you.

Thank the Lord for your family's blessings.

Giving From What Is Given

Give It Away

❖

Have you ever been at a sporting event where items were thrown into the stands for the fans? A baseball player might toss a baseball to a fan. Frisbees might soar into the crowd at the basketball game. What do fans usually do when things are tossed their way? If someone actually grabs something, he or she usually hangs on and doesn't let go. God gives out many gifts to his people, but he doesn't want his people to keep their gifts for themselves.

**Each of you should use whatever gift you have received
to serve others, as faithful stewards of God's grace
in its various forms. If anyone speaks, they should do so
as one who speaks the very words of God.
If anyone serves, they should do so
with the strength God provides,
so that in all things God may be praised
through Jesus Christ. 1 PETER 4:10,11**

Some have athletic talents. Some can speak beautiful prayers. Some are able to bake and cook well. Some can share their faith boldly. Don't selfishly hold onto the gifts and talents that God gave you as if it is a T-shirt shot into the grandstands. God wants you to recognize your ability and then use your talents faithfully to serve those he has placed in your life. He gives you words so you can proclaim Jesus to others. God gives you strength through your baptism to praise Jesus by giving away the gifts and using the talents he has given you.

- List some of your gifts and talents. How can you use them to serve others?

- What promises from the Bible give you strength to serve Jesus?

Ask God to give you opportunities to serve others in your home, at school, and at church.

God Uses Water

Higher Ground

❖

If the rivers flood, where do you go? Hopefully you get to higher ground. But what if even the highest peaks of the mountains were covered with water? God planned to flood the entire earth in order to destroy all of the unbelievers whose hearts were evil. There would be no higher ground that would be safe! Yet not everyone's heart was evil. Noah, his sons, and their wives believed in God's promise of a coming Savior. First, God would save them from the coming flood.

For forty days the flood kept coming on the earth, and as the waters increased they lifted the ark high above the earth. The waters rose and covered the mountains to a depth of more than fifteen cubits. GENESIS 7:17,20

Imagine—nothing but water covered the earth. There were no birds flying above and no green grass to tickle your toes. There was just water and an ark filled with animals and a godly family. Under the water there was evidence that God judges the wicked, but above the water there was evidence that God is gracious and merciful to sinners. Noah and his family found the high "ground" as they were being lifted by the water. Jesus is our high ground, our place of safety. He keeps us safe, not by means of an ark, but by his promises of forgiveness and love.

- Eight people were on the ark. What else did Noah take on the ark? How do you think those eight people felt, when the water started to lift the ark?

- God destroyed all those who were not on the ark. Why don't you need to be afraid when Jesus returns to judge the world?

Ask God to use you to share the good news of Jesus with those who do not believe.

God Uses Water

Salvation Provided

❖

After supper Gary would run to the freezer and grab the ice cream bars. Sometimes there was only one left. Because Gary was much taller, he would simply hold the last ice cream bar over his head to keep it safe from his younger sister Shelly. God wasn't trying to keep ice cream safe, instead, he wanted to keep Noah and his family safe from the life destroying flood. How did God keep them safe? The waters that destroyed the wicked unbelievers are the same waters that lifted the ark out of the reach of destruction. How does God save you?

**In it [the ark] only a few people, eight in all,
were saved through water,
and this water symbolizes baptism
that now saves you also. . . .
It saves you by the resurrection of Jesus Christ.** 1 PETER 3:20,21.

The rainbow is a reminder from God that he will not destroy the earth with another flood. Yet sin floods this world and our own hearts. We are born sinful and deserve to be punished in hell forever. God doesn't provide an ark to save you, but instead he gave his one and only Son to be your Savior. Your baptism isn't meant to wash dirt from your body but to wash sin from your soul. Your baptism connects you to Jesus who rose from the dead and promises that because he lives, you too live in him—and will live in him forever. Through the water and the Word you are saved!

- When were you baptized? What are some things you can do to remind yourself of your baptism every day?

- How can your baptism be a comfort to you every day?

Thank the Holy Spirit for connecting you to Jesus' promises through your baptism.

God Uses Water

There Will Be Water

❖

How many years did it take for Noah to build the ark? One hundred and twenty! How old was Noah when the flood came? Noah was six hundred years old! By building the ark, old Noah showed that his faith was very bold.

By faith Noah, when warned about things not yet seen, in holy fear built an ark to save his family. By his faith he condemned the world and became heir of the righteousness that is in keeping with faith. HEBREWS 11:7

"Hey, Noah! Where is the water?" The Bible doesn't tell us that Noah built the ark next to the ocean. The ark was probably built out on an open, dry plain. How foolish Noah must have looked to those who didn't take God seriously. Noah saw the flood coming, not with his eyes, but with his faith. Noah didn't dillydally around and say, "Aw, do I have to?" Noah believed, and by building the ark he preached a very powerful sermon to all those who didn't. The ark was a reminder to Noah and a warning to others that God is serious about sin and that he never fails to follow through on his promises. Noah believed in God's warning, but more importantly, he believed that God forgave him, loved him, and would save his family. Through faith, God gave Noah—and God gives you—his forgiveness and blessings in Jesus. Even though we can't always see, we can believe that what God says will always happen.

- How is the fear of an unbeliever and a believer different?

- Both Noah and you are heirs of righteousness through faith. What does that mean? How does this truth emphasize God's love and grace?

Pray for a bold faith that believes without seeing.

21

Grateful Hearts

The Right Response

❖

What do you think it was like on Noah's ark? What were the smells? What were the sounds? What is the first thing you would have done when you got off of the ark? Noah teaches us an important lesson by his response.

**Then Noah built an altar to the LORD and,
taking some of all the clean animals and clean birds,
he sacrificed burnt offerings on it.
The LORD smelled the pleasing aroma and said in his heart:
"Never again will I curse the ground because of humans,
even though every inclination of the human heart
is evil from childhood."** GENESIS 8:20,21

The first thing Noah did shows that he was totally dedicated to the Lord—he burned some of the clean animals as a sacrifice to God. Noah understood why God saved him. It wasn't because Noah was less of a sinner than others. God even says that human beings are evil from childhood. God saved Noah because he has compassion on sinners. God's love is so great that he even loves the unlovable—we call that grace. God loves you! How do you know? Noah could look at the wooden ark and marvel at how God shut its door and took care of him for many months. You can look at the wooden cross and marvel at how Jesus died for you so that you would be taken care of for an eternity. In Christ, God doesn't see you as evil but forgiven and holy. In Christ, you are saved.

- Explain what it means that God is merciful and gracious to you.

- You don't burn sacrifices to God. In what ways can you respond to Jesus' sacrifice for you?

Pray for a grateful heart that responds to God's grace and mercy.

Grateful Hearts

Where Do Your Thanks Go?

❖

Who are some people you often thank? How do you thank them? If you tell your grandparents thank you, you have to see them face-to-face or at least call them. If you want to thank your teacher, maybe you write her a note in your best penmanship. If a relative who sent you money for your birthday lives far away, you might write him a nice card and send it in the mail. But in order to give thanks, you have to have someone to call, someone to whom you can write a note or to whom you can send a card. The apostle Paul reminds us that we always have someone whom we can and should thank.

Always giving thanks to God the Father for everything, in the name of our Lord Jesus Christ. EPHESIANS 5:20

There is always a place to send your thanks! This passage reminds us of the promise that you have been saved in the name of Jesus. Christ washed away all your sin and removed the guilt that stood between you and God. Not only can you go to God, but you go to God as your Father. You are the child that he loves and likes. Your Father enjoys taking care of you and is happy to give you good things. The Father was happy to give to you his greatest gift, his one and only Son, who gives you reason to always give thanks.

- Paul tells us to always give thanks. Why can we give God thanks even during bad times and on days when things don't seem so good?

- How does having a thankful heart affect your attitude and mood?

Pray for a thankful heart.

23

Grateful Hearts

Taught to Be Bold

❖

Are you ever shy about asking for something? Do you ever hesitate to ask because you are afraid that the answer might be no? When Jesus taught his disciples to pray, he taught them to be bold. You too can be bold and confident that your heavenly Father will give to you everything you need.

Give us today our daily bread. MATTHEW 6:11

Did you ever wonder why Jesus teaches you to request daily bread? Wouldn't it be better if you had a weekly or even yearly supply? You then could go to the basement, the cupboards, or the garage and know that you have all that you need for the rest of the week or year. Jesus doesn't want you to be at peace or to be confident that everything is going to be all right because of *what* you have. He wants you to be confident that everything is going to be all right because of *who* you have. This short prayer teaches you to depend on God not once a week or once a year but every day. Your Father in heaven wants you to look to him for everything. If you are asking God to give you what you need every day, you then are reminded that you can give him thanks every day too. Not only can you rejoice that you have the Father who gives to you, but really it is the Father who has you and all of your needs in his almighty care.

- What are some needs that your family has?

- Why don't you ever have to be shy to ask God to give you what you need for your daily life?

Ask the Father to give you everything you need for today.

Powerful Promises

What Moves You?

❖

What do you like about your home? It is nice to have your own stuff. It is wonderful to have people you love and who love you. Would it be easy to move and leave everything behind? Abram did just that.

**The LORD had said to Abram,
"Go from your country, your people and
your father's household to the land I will show you."**
GENESIS 12:1

Why would Abram leave behind the friends he knew and the family he loved? Why would he leave behind some of his inheritance and the business that he built? Did he just feel that it was the right thing to do? No! Abram didn't move because of the feelings he had. Abram moved because of God's promise. Faith and feelings aren't the same thing. Feelings rely on what is inside of you; faith relies on what comes from the Almighty God. Abram had fingers of faith that gripped the promises of God tightly. Faith simply says that God's Word is true and his promises can't be broken. Abram moved because of a promise that he couldn't see with his eyes but could see with his heart. God has given you many promises. He promised that you are forgiven and that he loves you. These promises have created faith in your heart and have moved you to believe.

- Faith is not the same as having a feeling. What does faith rely on? Why can't you always trust your feelings?

- If your faith holds to God's promises, what is important for you to do and to know?

Ask God to give you a mind that can memorize his promises and a heart to trust them.

Powerful Promises

A Promise for Everyone

❖

Birthday parties can be very fun. Usually there are games, presents, and cake. Many times there aren't only presents for the birthday boy or girl but for everyone. Have you ever given or received a birthday treat bag? God gave Abram many gifts, but God didn't forget you either. You have a promise that you can take with you and will be with you forever.

**"I will make you into a great nation,
and I will bless you;
I will make your name great,
and you will be a blessing.
I will bless those who bless you,
and whoever curses you I will curse;
and all peoples on earth
will be blessed through you."** GENESIS 12:2,3

Why was it an incredible miracle that Abram even became a nation? Abram was 75 years old when he received this promise from God. But that doesn't mean he and his wife had children right away. 25 years went by before he had his first son with his wife Sarah. She was 90 years old and Abram was 100! Abram received an incredible gift through his son; you did too. Many years after Abram' son was born, Jesus was born from Abram's family. That is why God promised that all peoples on earth would be blessed through Abram. God didn't forget about blessing you. God the Father gave you his Son who wouldn't only bring joy and happiness but also forgiveness, peace, and eternal life. This promise was for Abram, for you, and everyone.

- Pick out other promises that God gave to Abram. How did God keep those promises?

Thank the Lord for always keeping his promises.

Powerful Promises

It Is Worth Repeating

❖

Has anyone ever repeated something he already told you? It can be annoying when someone keeps repeating himself. The Lord repeats himself not to annoy you but to strengthen you. It is a gift to hear God tell you every day that he loves you and forgives you in Jesus. If God ever repeats himself, just listen and believe.

Abram traveled through the land as far as the site of the great tree of Moreh at Shechem. At that time the Canaanites were in the land. The Lord appeared to Abram and said, "To your offspring I will give this land." So he built an altar there to the Lord, who had appeared to him. GENESIS 12:6,7

Abram moved from his home because God promised to give him a new land. When Abram arrived, the land was already taken. How would you have felt? The Lord didn't appear to Abram to apologize for making a mistake or breaking a promise. God doesn't make mistakes or break promises. The Lord appeared to him to repeat his promise. The land would belong to Abram's family someday. God repeats his promises to you because through his promises he strengthens your faith and reassures you that he cares. He chases away your doubts when you hear his Word. Abram's doubts were gone. He showed that by worshiping the Lord. Whether hearing the same promises or new ones, thank God for repeating himself.

- In the beginning of a worship service, God promises you forgiveness through the pastor. What do you usually do after you hear that promise?

- You know many of God's promises. Why do you need them repeated?

Pray that you would never tire of God's repeated promises.

Royal Promises

The Blood-Red Thread of Jesus

❖

Many people like to study their family tree and understand who their relatives were. Who are some of your relatives? How far back can you go? How many of Jesus' relatives can you list? Really, it is quite amazing that we can even ask such a question about our God.

> **Judah, your brothers will praise you;**
> **your hand will be on the neck of your enemies;**
> **your father's sons will bow down to you.**
> **The scepter will not depart from Judah,**
> **nor the ruler's staff from between his feet.** GENESIS 49:8,10

All nations would be blessed through Abraham because from his family the Savior would be born. The promise of a Savior was passed down to Isaac and then to Jacob. But who received the promise after Jacob? Judah's brothers would praise him because from his family the Messiah would be born. Isn't it a marvel that God has a family record? God, who is invisible, loved you so much that he became visible by being born of Mary. The eternal God, who has no beginning and no end, humbled himself and lived in time. The God who created the earth with the Word, sent the Word to humbly live on earth so that you could have the hope of living in his kingdom. Jesus does reign over all things for your good and rules your heart through the gospel.

- This is the first promise that the Savior would come from a royal family. How did Jesus live as our King when he lived here on earth?

- List some specific things that Jesus rules over which give you comfort?

Pray that Jesus would make your heart his royal throne by keeping you connected to the gospel.

28

Royal Promises

Really Ruling

❖

What do you think of when you hear that a king rules? Why would a king want to have armies, castles, and large territories? Jesus is your King, but he didn't wear royal robes, have a fancy throne, or have armies with battle chariots driving for him. Yet Jesus fought your battle against sin and gives to you a royal promise.

> **The other criminal rebuked him. "Don't you fear God,"
> he said, "since you are under the same sentence?
> We are punished justly, for we are getting what our deeds
> deserve. But this man has done nothing wrong."
> Then he said, "Jesus, remember me when you
> come into your kingdom." Jesus answered him,
> "Truly I tell you, today you will be with me in paradise."**
> LUKE 23:40-43

Your king fought for you without lifting a sword or shooting a bow. Jesus fought for you by having himself lifted up on the cross even though he did nothing wrong. Jesus died for your wrongs and on the cross received the punishment that you deserved. Why would he do this? It is because of grace! Grace is the love that begins in Jesus. He showed his love by making the cross the throne from which he ruled! He forgave your sin and on the cross conquered death! Your King promises that you are in his kingdom and that you will be with him in paradise forever.

- As an individual, what are some ways you can show that Jesus rules your heart and life? As a family?

- How does Jesus' promise help us find joy even in death?

Praise God for the full and free forgiveness that he gives to you.

Royal Promises

King of Rescue

❖

Why do ships have lifeboats? Why do cars have airbags? Why do pools have flotation devices and long poles with a hook on the end? Bad things sometimes happen and people need to be rescued. The darkness of sin completely filled our hearts. There wasn't even a little bit of light shining in us. There was no good living in us. We didn't need help—we needed complete rescue!

**He has rescued us from the dominion of darkness
and brought us into the kingdom
of the Son he loves, in whom we have redemption,
the forgiveness of sins.** COLOSSIANS 1:13,14

If we weren't originally in Jesus' kingdom, to whose kingdom did we belong? It is frightening to think that we were slaves to sin and ruled by the darkness of Satan. Heaven wasn't our home, but death in hell was. We don't need a helper—we need a Savior. In Jesus we have the Savior we need. He rescued you by paying for your sin, not with gold or silver, but with his holy precious blood. Jesus pulled you from the darkness of death into the wonderful light of forgiveness which gives to you life now and forever.

If you pay for a piece of candy, to whom does that candy belong? Jesus paid for you. To whom do you now belong? Satan does not control you. Sin does not enslave you and death has no hold on you. The power and rule of Christ lives in your heart, and you are a part of Jesus' glorious kingdom.

- Jesus is the king of our hearts. How does that guide you when you watch TV, surf the internet, or decide what video game to play?

Thank Jesus for redemption and forgiveness.

Lessons From Young Moses

My Protector

❖

How do you protect yourself from scary things? Nightlights help by chasing the creepy darkness from our rooms. We wear seatbelts when riding in the car and helmets when riding a bike, all to be safe. But you can't take your nightlight with you out of the house and your helmet can't protect you from everything. God is, however, with you in the dark and as you go out of your home to work or play. God protects you by using other people and things in this world to guard you from danger.

She [Pharaoh's daughter] saw the basket among the reeds and sent her female slave to get it. She opened it and saw the baby. He was crying, and she felt sorry for him. "This is one of the Hebrew babies," she said. She named him Moses, saying, "I drew him out of the water." EXODUS 2:5,6,10

God the Father didn't cause the basket to miraculously rise up in the air out of the reach of the crocodiles. He didn't surround Moses in a protective bubble, yet the Lord protected Moses. There are many scary things that we have to face in this life, yet we don't face them alone. Our eyes cannot see God, but the Bible does tell us that God is always with us, and he shows us that he uses other people and things around us to protect his people—to protect you!

- Try to retell some of the details of the Bible lesson about baby Moses (Exodus 2). What did God use to keep Moses safe from danger?

- What are some things that scare you? How does God keep you safe from physical and spiritual dangers?

Praise God for the love and safety that he daily provides you.

Lessons From Young Moses

A Treasure Given

❖

Have you ever been sad to leave home? What could make you sad or worried to leave home? Many tears are cried by moms and dads on the first day of kindergarten or even the first day of college. Parents give kids big hugs or maybe even cell phones so that they can talk to their children when they are away. But what is even more important to take with you when you leave home?

When the child grew older, she [Moses' mother] took him to Pharaoh's daughter and he became her son. She named him Moses, saying, "I drew him out of the water." One day, after Moses had grown up, he went out to where his own people were and watched them at their hard labor. EXODUS 2:10,11.

How do you think Moses' mom felt when she took her little boy to live with the princess of Egypt? Moses didn't leave home with a cell phone, he had something better. When Moses was growing up, his mother told him about the true God. He knew he wasn't an Egyptian who worshiped the sun and other false gods. Moses knew he belonged to God's chosen people. It might be very scary to be away from parents, but a child who leaves home knowing the true God is never alone! When you leave your home, you can leave knowing you belong to Jesus.

- What are some things your family can do to make your home the best classroom for learning about God?

- How does it help to know that when we leave home, we leave as God's people?

Pray that God continues to make your home a place of learning and prayer.

Lessons From Young Moses

Growing Up With Purpose

❖

What are some things you are learning or have learned in school? How can you use what you have learned to serve God? Your purpose in life is to use the talents and wisdom the Lord gives to you to serve him.

Moses was educated in all the wisdom of the Egyptians and was powerful in speech and action. ACTS 7:22

God used the princess of Egypt to rescue Moses from the Nile River. After Moses was old enough to live in the palace, he was educated in the finest schools in Egypt. Moses witnessed how powerful leaders ran a country. He learned how to think and how to apply math. Moses worked hard in order to put sentences together and speak well. God gave him the gift of education and then used Moses to lead the chosen people of Israel to the Promised Land. When you are at school learning from your teacher or at home learning from a parent or grandparent, God is giving you the job to learn about his creation and understand the world around you. God called you to be his child through the waters of your baptism and is preparing you to serve him in this world. You may not have all of the wisdom of the Egyptians, but you do have the wisdom and love of Jesus, which empowers you to serve him in all that you do.

- Moses wrote the first five books of the Bible. He had skills to write, read, and lead. What are some skills that God has given to you?

- How can you use your talents to serve the Lord in the following areas of your life?
  - School—
  - Church—
  - Community—
  - Home—

Ask God to use your gifts and talents to give him praise and honor.

God Is for Us

Help Is on the Way!

❖

What is a worrywart? If you touch the warts someone has on his fingers, there is a chance that the warts can spread to you. Why isn't worry a good thing? What would happen to your worries if God promised he would help you and that he would even fight for you?

Moses answered the people, "Do not be afraid. Stand firm and you will see the deliverance the Lord will bring you today. . . . The Lord will fight for you; you need only to be still." EXODUS 14:13,14

The Israelites were in a worrisome situation! Behind them angry Egyptians were approaching and in front of them the Red Sea made it impossible for them to run away. The Israelites were certain they were going to die because they didn't believe God could help.

What has been troubling and worrying you? Have you become so focused on all of the challenges at school or troubles with your friends, or are you so afraid of what might happen in the future that you have lost your focus on the God you can't see? God tells you to be still, to be silent and trust in him. God's help is on the way. Your God fights for you and will deliver you. How do you know? You can't see him, but God does speak to you through his Word! He promises salvation. Jesus' cross proves he fought and will fight for you.

- What have you been afraid of lately? List some of the promises the Lord has given you, which can drive your fears away.

- How does God continue to fight for you?

Pray that Jesus' promise to deliver you brings peace to your heart.

God Is for Us

To the Left and to the Right

❖

Have you ever visited an aquarium or looked into a fish tank? What strange or interesting things did you see? Moses and the Israelites were able to venture through one of the most spectacular aquariums. This aquarium didn't have large walls of glass made by man; instead it had large walls of water piled up by God!

All that night the LORD drove the sea back with a strong east wind and turned it into dry land. The waters were divided, and the Israelites went through the sea on dry ground, with a wall of water on their right and on their left. EXODUS 14:21,22

What did God's people see? Maybe they saw sea creatures and fish swimming by. Maybe an Israelite boy paused to pick up a rock and a girl bent low to pick up a shell. We don't know everything that they saw, but we do know the most important thing that they saw. When they looked to the right, they saw God's power and protection. When they looked to the left, they were reminded that God was keeping his promise to save them. The Lord did the impossible so that the Israelites could see that he was almighty and serious about never breaking a promise. The God who parted the Red Sea is also the God who will never break his promise to lead you through life and keep you safe.

- What are some symbols or objects that you can look at to remind you of God's love and power?

- God used natural means to drive back the water. What natural means does God use to take care of you?

Thank God that he uses his power to save his people.

35

God Is for Us

Wow, Power!

❖

Imagine standing near train tracks when a train traveling 60 miles an hour and hauling 130 cars is going by. What would you feel? Now imagine if you were standing on the tracks. What would your only option be? Run! When things are bigger than we are and more powerful than we are, it is easy to be afraid. How should we feel about God who is bigger and more powerful than we are?

That day the Lord saved Israel from the hands of the Egyptians, and Israel saw the Egyptians lying dead on the shore. And when the Israelites saw the mighty hand of the Lord displayed against the Egyptians, the people feared the Lord and put their trust in him and in Moses his servant. EXODUS 14:30,31

The Egyptians tried to *stand on the tracks* against God and lost badly. The entire army was now dead. God's people were safe and alive! When they saw that the Red Sea was parted for them and then closed upon the Egyptians, they quickly realized God was awesome. They realized God was much, much bigger and more powerful than they were. Israel feared the Lord and put their trust in him.

God's grace doesn't put you on the train tracks, but as forgiven children who believe in Jesus, the Holy Spirit has put you on the correct side of the tracks in order to stand in awe of God and fear him. Marvel that God uses his power for us and that though he is much, much bigger, Jesus humbled himself to save us. Wow!

- What are some awesome miracles that show the power of God? What are some awesome things God has done in your life?

Praise God for using his awesome power to save and help you.

God Provides

Great Grumblers!

❖

Do you like to listen to others when they are grumbling? Why not? The Israelites were freed from slavery in Egypt by God who displayed his almighty power. Yet they were great grumblers!

The Israelites said . . . , "If only we had died by the LORD's hand in Egypt! There we sat around pots of meat and ate all the food we wanted, but you have brought us out into this desert to starve this entire assembly to death." Moses . . . said, "You are not grumbling against us, but against the LORD." EXODUS 16:3,8

The Israelites forgot what they had and focused on what they didn't have. Does that ever happen to you? Instead of giving thanks for your loving parent who gives you food, have you ever complained about the food you have? Have you ever grumbled over the clothes that you don't have instead of being happy about what is in your closet? Parents and teachers aren't the only ones who think that grumbles sound ugly—God does too. When you grumble, you fail to remember that God gave you what you need. When you complain, you fail to trust that God will provide you with what is best. Your Lord is the God of love who rejoices in giving to you. The Father loves you so much that he gave you his Son who lived without ever grumbling, even though he owned very little. Jesus loves you so much that he didn't grumble on the cross. He knew you needed him and the forgiveness that only he could provide for all of your grumbles.

- Instead of thinking about what you don't have, make a list of all the good things you do have.

Praise God for forgiving your grumbles.

God Provides

Special Delivery

❖

Did you pick up your cornflakes or breakfast pastry out on the lawn today? Many people live by the five second rule: If something falls on the floor, it is all right to eat it if it was there less than five seconds. Maybe you have been told not to eat something that falls on the ground. After the Israelites complained that they had no food, the Lord graciously gave them a special delivery that they could pick up from the desert floor.

In the morning there was a layer of dew around the camp. When the dew was gone, thin flakes like frost on the ground appeared on the desert floor. . . . Moses said to them, "It is the bread the LORD has given you to eat." EXODUS 16:13-15

There were no superstores in the Israelites' camp and no food trucks selling walking tacos. God's people needed food. It is estimated that around two million people left Egypt and now lived in a big desert camp! Think about how many semitrucks full of food it would take every day to feed all of the people. But God didn't need trucks or trailers. After the dew was gone in the morning, the Lord used his power to provide bread from heaven. Even though you most likely don't pick up your food on the lawn, God also provides you with everything you need for body and life. He doesn't forget and knows what you need. Through Jesus he provides you with a home in heaven. He also provides all the other things you need. Trust in the Lord for he loves you.

- In the Lord's Prayer we ask God to give us our daily bread. What are we asking for?

- God shows that he can provide in miraculous ways. In what natural ways does God provide for you?

Ask God to bless your family with what is needed.

God Provides

The Better Bread

❖

What are some things that you need to live? You can survive about three days without water and up to three weeks without food! Food and water are essential for your body to live, but you need more than just food and water to live spiritually. Jesus teaches us that he is the better bread.

Jesus said to them, "Very truly I tell you, it is not Moses who has given you the bread from heaven, but it is my Father who gives you the true bread from heaven. For the bread of God is the bread that comes down from heaven and gives life to the world." JOHN 6:32,33

The Jews who were listening to Jesus wanted more bread to eat. They pointed back to the manna their ancestors ate and wanted Jesus to provide like Moses did. They were mistaken over who provided the manna. God the Father gave the necessary food for the Israelites to survive, and he provided even better bread so that all can survive spiritually. Have you ever found yourself more focused on what you can get in this world than on what is stored up for you in heaven? It is easier to understand what you want than it is to understand what you need. Praise God the Father for providing us with Jesus, who is the better bread. Jesus' forgiveness is what we need daily, and through your baptism and the Word, you have that forgiveness. With Jesus being the better bread, you will live forever.

- Often families make a grocery list of the things that they need. What can you do as a family to make sure that you are receiving the better bread that you need daily?

Thank Jesus for being the Savior who came from heaven.

The Law of God

The Purpose of God's Law

❖

If you keep the lights out in your room, is it harder to see the mess under the bed or in the closet? God's law is like turning on the lights inside of our hearts in order to see the mess of sin.

No one will be declared righteous in God's sight by the works of the law; rather, through the law we become conscious of our sin. ROMANS 3:20

Turning on the lights in your room allows you to see dirty clothes on the floor, gum wrappers under your bed, and dust on the shelves. What do you need to do when you see those things? No, you cannot shut the door and run away. You need to start cleaning. God's laws allow us to see the mess sin makes in our lives. The light of God's law reveals that we haven't always loved God with our whole heart and we haven't loved others perfectly. We deserve to go to hell because of our sin! Can we simply shut the door and run away from our mess? No. Can we clean up our sin on our own? No. The law shows us our sin in order to show us that we need Jesus. Jesus isn't just a helper in life; he is our Savior who gives us life. Jesus never sinned, not even once! He lived perfectly so that through faith his perfection would become your perfection. You are holy and right with God because of Jesus!

- Can a person go to heaven by trying really hard to obey God's commandments?

- In your own words, explain why you can be confident that you are saved.

Pray that the law of God always makes you see your need for Jesus.

The Law of God

The Law Giver

❖

Through whom did God give the laws to the Israelites? How many commandments does Scripture say there are? God gave the Ten Commandments through Moses, but why did God give the commandments? The words God spoke before he gave his commandments help us answer that question.

God spoke all these words: "I am the LORD your God, who brought you out of Egypt, out of the land of slavery." EXODUS 20:1,2

Did God give the Ten Commandments to his people so that they could earn his favor? No! He already showed them incredible grace by delivering them from Egypt, the land of slavery. God introduces himself as the LORD. This is the special name that God uses when he wants us to remember him as the God who makes gracious promises and always keeps them. The Lord saved his people physically and promised to save them from sin by sending them a Savior. The Ten Commandments are not meant to be a burden. God doesn't give us his commands to enslave us again. The Lord gives us his commandments so that we can show our love for Jesus and thank him for saving us. The love that God shows us causes us to want to obey his will.

- Is it easier to obey someone who is angry or someone who is kind? Why?

- The Lord didn't rescue us from Egypt, but he did rescue us from slavery. Who or what held us as slaves?

- How did Jesus rescue each of us from our slave masters?

Pray for the Holy Spirit to give you a heart of joy that is willing to obey God's will out of thanksgiving and praise.

The Law of God

Jesus Is for Me!

❖

Are you a little sinful or very sinful? God's Word commands us to be perfect (Matthew 5:48). If you are wondering if you are perfect in every way, just ask the people who know you best if you are. God demands that you be perfect, and if you are not, you deserve to go to hell! You can't perfectly obey God's laws, but Jesus was perfect for you.

When the set time had fully come, God sent his Son, born of a woman, born under the law, to redeem those under the law, that we might receive adoption to sonship. GALATIANS 4:4,5

When the time was absolutely perfect, Jesus was born of the virgin Mary to live under the law. As God's Son and as true man, Jesus followed the rules and commands of his Father perfectly. Not once did Jesus lie, cheat, steal, hurt, talk back to his mom, or hate anyone. Not once! Instead, Jesus loved, was kind, gentle, perfectly patient, and always respectful. God demands you to be perfect in order to be with him forever in heaven. You aren't perfect by yourself, but you aren't by yourself. Jesus is your Savior who was born for you. Through faith in him, his perfection is now your perfection. Be perfect! You are, in Christ Jesus!

- Jesus' holiness is wrapped around you like a brilliant white robe. When the Father looks at you, he sees Jesus' perfection. How can you show God your thankfulness for such an incredible gift?

- You are set free from sin! You can't and don't need to depend on obeying the commandments in order to be with Jesus in heaven. Why is this good news?

Thank God for sending his Son to be perfect for you!

Piles of Lessons

Patiently Trust

❖

Do you ever get impatient? Have you ever tried to peek at a birthday or Christmas gift by pealing back the wrapping paper just a little bit? It is sometimes hard to wait patiently, especially when something good is coming. God promised the Israelites many good things, but he also taught them an important lesson through waiting.

**Then the Lord said to Joshua,
"See, I have delivered Jericho into your hands. . . .
March around the city once with all the armed men.
Do this for six days. . . . On the seventh day,
march around the city seven times."** JOSHUA 6:2-4

Did you notice that the Lord told the Israelites to march around the city for an entire week? Would their marching cause the walls to fall down? No, the Lord was going to conquer the city by causing the walls to tumble over. Why then did he make them wait? Every day that they marched, God wanted his people to put their hope in his promise that he would give the city of Jericho into their hands. The Lord wanted his people to grow in their trust in what God would do for them. God wanted his people to have Jericho, but even more than that, God wanted his people to have a stronger faith in what he would do. Trust that God will always keep his promises to you, even if he asks you to wait.

- What are some promises God has made that you are still waiting for?

- The Israelites put their faith into action by marching around the city because they were confident God would conquer Jericho. How can you put your faith into action as you wait for the above promises to be fulfilled?

Pray that the Holy Spirit keeps your faith strong in his promises.

Piles of Lessons

The Lord Wants You!

❖

Were you there when God created the world? Were you there when Jesus died for the world? God created all things and he saved the world without anyone's help. The Lord doesn't need you, but the Bible teaches that God wants you to be involved in his work!

On the seventh day, they got up at daybreak and marched around the city seven times in the same manner, except that on that day they circled the city seven times. When the trumpets sounded, the army shouted, and at the sound of the trumpet, when the men gave a loud shout, the wall collapsed; so everyone charged straight in, and they took the city. JOSHUA 6:15,20

The almighty Lord didn't need the vibrations from the marching feet. God didn't need the trumpet sounds and the loud shouts for the walls to collapse. But God wanted his people to be involved with this incredible miracle and victory over Jericho. You need the Lord on your side, and God wants you to be involved with the incredible work he is still doing in the world. People need to hear about Jesus. You can tell them. Jesus wants to work through your gifts and talents so you can do amazing things for him and with him.

- The Lord uses your gifts and talents to do amazing things, whether you think those things are big or small. What are some ways God uses your gifts and talents to do his work in the following areas of your life?
  - Home—

  - School—

  - Church—

  - Work—

- How does knowing that God rejoices in using you to do his work change your attitude about serving?

Ask the Lord to use you to serve and honor him in everything you do.

Piles of Lessons

Totally Dedicated

❖

When the Israelites conquered Jericho, they were to destroy everything. They weren't to take any gold, silver, or anything else for themselves, but they were to give it to the Lord. Why would God want them to take nothing for themselves, especially if it was just going to be burned up?

**They devoted the city to the Lord. . . .
Then they burned the whole city and everything in it,
but they put the silver and gold and the articles of bronze
and iron into the treasury of the Lord's house.** JOSHUA 6:21,24

God knew that sinful hearts fall in love with things instead of loving the Creator who made all things. The Lord didn't want the Israelites' hearts to be attached to stuff in the Promised Land. God wanted his people to be attached to him. You haven't been asked to rush into Jericho, but you do live in a world where many people worship false gods and earthly treasures. God doesn't want you to love things but to love him above *all* things. God gave Jericho to the Israelites and they were to devote everything to him. You don't have a Jericho filled with riches, but you do have Jesus who forgives you and promises that he is a treasure worth much more than all the gold in this world. He promises that your treasure is in heaven with him.

- What are some things that can distract you from being devoted to the Lord?

- God didn't need the Israelites to collect money for him. He is the Creator who has all things! What did God want from his people and from you?

Pray that the Holy Spirit keeps your heart attached to Jesus through the gospel.

Serve the Lord

Committed

❖

Has anyone, perhaps a coach or your parents, ever given you a pep talk? What did they say to motivate you to play harder or to clean up your room better? God not only has given us a pep talk about serving him, but he also gives us powerful motivation for serving.

Then I sent Moses and Aaron, and I afflicted the Egyptians by what I did there, and I brought you out. When I brought your people out of Egypt . . . JOSHUA 24:5,6

Did you notice what word was repeated in these verses? If you were to read verses 3-13 in Joshua chapter 24, you would see that God repeated the word *I* 18 times. The Lord wanted the Israelites to understand that they were his chosen people because *he* chose them. They were freed from slavery in Egypt because of the miracles *he* did. They were living in the promised land because *he* destroyed their enemies and gave them the land. When it comes to the Israelites' rescue and your salvation, it is all God's doing. God rescued them from slavery and God rescued you from the slavery of sin through Jesus Christ. Why? Because God is filled with grace. The Lord loves you unconditionally. The Lord was committed to his Old Testament people and would not break his promises. Every time you look at a cross it is a reminder that Jesus was committed to saving you! You serve the Lord, not to win his love, but you serve because he freely gave his love to you.

- This section of God's Word reviews how God showed his people love and commitment. What parts of a Christian worship service remind you of the love Jesus has for his people?

Thank the Lord for his grace in saving you.

Serve the Lord

Stubbornly Serve

❖

Is being stubborn usually a bad or a good thing? The answer to that question depends on why you are being stubborn. When it comes to serving the Lord, Joshua teaches that being stubborn is the only way.

If serving the LORD seems undesirable to you, then choose for yourselves this day whom you will serve, whether the gods your ancestors served beyond the Euphrates, or the gods of the Amorites, in whose land you are living. But as for me and my household, we will serve the LORD. JOSHUA 24:15

Joshua knew that God's chosen people would be tempted to follow idols and false gods. He gave them the choice to worship any god that they chose. However, Joshua already had his mind and heart set on fearing and serving the Lord. Joshua believed that no other god could rescue him. Only the true God could. No other god gave Joshua the promise of forgiveness and eternal life. No other god lived, loved, and cared for him like the Lord! The same is true for you. Even though Joshua lived about 3,500 years ago, Joshua's God is your God. The living Lord doesn't change, and that is why Joshua stubbornly said that he wouldn't either. There are many people who love false gods and idols, but there is only one Lord who loves you. Stubbornly serve Jesus and stand in awe of the salvation he freely gave you by dying on the cross.

- How is your family going to serve the Lord?

- How can the members of a family encourage one another to stay strong in the faith when so many in the world don't believe?

Ask the Holy Spirit to give you a willing spirit to serve.

Serve the Lord

No Such Thing as *Kind of* Serving

❖

How would you feel if your family told you that they kind of loved you? It would hurt! God doesn't want his people to kind of love him but to love and serve him above all things!

"We too will serve the LORD**, because he is our God."**
Joshua said to the people, "You are not able to serve the LORD**.**
He is a holy God; he is a jealous God.
He will not forgive your rebellion and your sins."
JOSHUA 24:18,19

The Israelites agreed to serve the Lord! You would think that Joshua would clap and holler with joy, but he doesn't. His words seem negative and sour. Why would he tell them that they were unable to serve God. Joshua was teaching them that if they chose to serve the Lord, they needed to be serious about it. God doesn't accept a heart that kind of, sort of loves him once in a while. The Lord is a jealous God and wants you to love him above all things. The Lord desires to have all of your love—all of your worship and praise. He wants you to be his so much that he even died for you. Jesus gave his very life for you, and because of his grace, you are able to give your life in service to him now and forever.

- How are you tempted to kind of worship the Lord on Sundays?

- Think about Jesus' perfect life. What did he do that shows he always worshiped and trusted in his Father perfectly for you?

Ask God to forgive you for the times when you kind of served him.

The Lord Is My Strength

Big Problems Require a Big God

❖

How would you feel if you had to fight the boxing champion of the world? Would you forfeit the fight? Would you run the other way? The Israelites faced a champion who wanted to fight them. Everyone was too afraid—everyone except David.

A champion named Goliath . . . came out of the Philistine camp. His height was six cubits and a span. Whenever the Israelites saw the man, they all fled from him in great fear. David said to Saul, "Your servant will go and fight him. . . . Your servant has killed both the lion and the bear. . . . The LORD who rescued me from the paw of the lion and the paw of the bear will rescue me from the hand of this Philistine." 1 SAMUEL 17:4,24,32,36,37

Goliath's body armor weighed 125 pounds! David, however, wasn't impressed by Goliath. David didn't put his hope in his own height or how many pounds of armor he could strap to his body. David put his hope in the Lord. You might be facing giant-sized challenges. If you put your hope in your own ability, there is a good chance that you will be afraid. Instead, put your hope in Jesus. Take your worries to the Almighty God who can help you. Jesus delivered you from more than a roaring lion or bear; he delivered you from sin and death! The Lord has destroyed your enemies and has rescued you from hell. Depend on Jesus to rescue you from challenges. Blessed are they who hope in the Lord!

- What challenges are you facing?

- How does David's boldness motivate you to face your fears and problems?

Ask God to be your strength as you face giant problems.

The Lord Is My Strength

The Lord's Hand and Mine

❖

Have you ever heard someone say, "Everything is in the Lord's hands"? Jesus certainly rules all things, but that doesn't mean we stop working hard. God works through what you do and uses your abilities to accomplish what he desires. David understood this. He didn't just run onto the battlefield and wait for the Lord to strike the giant down. David prepared himself for battle and trusted that the Lord would bless his efforts.

Then [David] took his staff in his hand, chose five smooth stones from the stream, put them in the pouch of his shepherd's bag and, with his sling in his hand, approached the Philistine.
1 SAMUEL 17:40

What is God's job in your life? God is the one who makes promises to you and keeps those promises. What is your job? Your job is to trust God's promises and then use the gifts God has given you. Trust that you are in the Lord's hands and also trust that the Lord is going to bless the work that your hands do. David ran onto the battlefield believing God would bless his efforts and preparation. God loves you. Be confident that the almighty Lord's blessings are coming to you. Especially important is the blessing of heaven.

- What are some tasks that God has given you to do?

- God uses your gifts and talents to bring you blessings. What are some ways God is going to bless you through your hard work and preparation?

Pray that the Lord blesses the use of your gifts and talents.

The Lord Is My Strength

The Reason to Fight

❖

Why do teams play hard? Why do students work hard at school? Why do your best? Some play for the trophy. Some like to have bragging rights. Some look forward to the reward when they bring home a good report card. But why do Christians do what they do?

David said to [Goliath], "You come against me with sword and spear and javelin, but I come against you in the name of the LORD Almighty. . . . This very day I will give the carcasses of the Philistine army to the birds and the wild animals, and the whole world will know that there is a God in Israel."
1 SAMUEL 17:45,46

David would have bragging rights if he killed Goliath. But David didn't want bragging rights for himself—he wanted bragging rights for the Lord. Why did the young shepherd boy fight the giant with a stone and a sling? David wanted to show that the Lord Almighty was fighting for Israel. It is a sin to boast about what you can do and how great you are. Jesus humbled himself on the cross to forgive you for the sin of pride. Jesus' forgiveness now moves you to boast in him. Use your talents to show that the Lord is at work in your heart and through your actions.

- The Israelites and the Philistines put their trust in weapons and soldiers. How was David different?

- David fought Goliath so everyone would know the Lord was fighting for his people. How can others see that you are fighting for the Lord?

Ask God to use you to proclaim his power and promises to others.

A Hot Situation

Only One God

❖

What would you do if you were forced to worship someone or something other than God? Continue to pray that the Lord never puts you in that situation, but know that believers once were. And some believers today are mistreated because of their faith in Jesus.

**King Nebuchadnezzar made an image of gold,
sixty cubits high and six cubits wide, and set it up on the plain
of Dura in the province of Babylon. Then the herald loudly
proclaimed, "Nations and peoples of every language,
this is what you are commanded to do: As soon as you hear
the sound of the horn, flute, zither, lyre, harp, pipe and
all kinds of music, you must fall down and worship the image
of gold that King Nebuchadnezzar has set up.
Whoever does not fall down and worship will immediately
be thrown into a blazing furnace."** DANIEL 3:1,4-6.

If anyone would bow down to the golden statue, they would be breaking the First Commandment: "You shall have no other gods." Every commandment that God gives to us protects something that God treasures. God doesn't ever want his glory and praise to be given to anyone or anything else. Nebuchadnezzar was putting himself in the place of God when he commanded people to sin by giving glory to a statue. The First Commandment teaches us to fear God above all things. This means believers should be afraid to do anything that would dishonor God or steal his glory, even if their refusal to sin would result in being thrown into a fiery furnace.

- You are not threatened with being thrown into a fiery furnace. What are some threats that tempt you to dishonor God?

- How can you show that you respect God?

Pray that God gives you boldness to fear him above all things.

A Hot Situation

Fearless Trust

❖

Think of some times when you were afraid. What did you do? There are going to be times when you are afraid and find yourself facing difficult situations. Three men give us an example of what we can do.

Furious with rage, Nebuchadnezzar summoned Shadrach, Meshach and Abednego. . . . Nebuchadnezzar said to them, "Is it true . . . that you do not serve my gods or worship the image of gold I have set up? . . . If you do not worship it, you will be thrown immediately into a blazing furnace."

Shadrach, Meshach and Abednego replied to him, "If we are thrown into the blazing furnace, the God we serve is able to deliver us from it, and he will deliver us from Your Majesty's hand. But even if he does not, we want you to know, Your Majesty, that we will not serve your gods or worship the image of gold you have set up." DANIEL 3:13-18

King Nebuchadnezzar was going to *barbeque* them if they didn't worship the golden statue. But no threat or scary situation would change the heart of these three faithful men. Why? They trusted in God above all things because the Lord controls every detail of life! They trusted that God could save them from the fiery furnace. But if it were not his will, they were willing to lose their lives instead of worshiping a false god. These three friends were fearless because they trusted that God was always faithful.

- Shadrach, Meshach, and Abednego were willing to die for God. Why do you think they were willing to do that?

- What does this Bible lesson teach you to do in scary situations?

Ask the Holy Spirit to drive worries from your heart with his powerful promises.

A Hot Situation

The True King Revealed

❖

Have you ever played a game to see who would be the champion of driveway basketball, Go Fish, or Mario Kart? Competition is a test to see who is the best and most skilled at a game. What happens when God is challenged to see who is the best and most powerful king?

[Nebuchadnezzar] ordered the furnace heated seven times hotter than usual and commanded some of the strongest soldiers in his army to tie up Shadrach, Meshach and Abednego and throw them into the blazing furnace. He said, "Look! I see four men walking around in the fire, unbound and unharmed, and the fourth looks like a son of the gods." . . .

Shadrach, Meshach and Abednego came out of the fire, and the satraps, prefects, governors and royal advisors . . . saw that the fire had not harmed their bodies, nor was a hair of their heads singed; their robes were not scorched, and there was no smell of fire on them. DANIEL 3:19,20,25-27

Shadrach, Meshach, and Abednego trusted that God loved them and had given them promises of salvation. These men showed that they loved God above all things by their willingness to be burned alive! Nebuchadnezzar thought that he was in control of the situation and challenged God when he threw God's people into the fiery furnace. But the men's clothes didn't even smell like smoke when they came out of the furnace. The Lord protected his faithful sons and showed Nebuchadnezzar that he was no contest for the Almighty God, the true King.

- Many leaders and bullies think they are in control. How does it help you in your life to understand that God is King over all?

- What awesome message did this miraculous escape proclaim to those standing near?

Thank God for revealing his power and care for his people.

Thanks Living

Do What I Do

❖

"Blain, why do you pull your cowboy hat down so tight?" He answered, "Because my daddy does." "Blain, why do you want to ride a scary bull at the rodeo?" He answered, "Because my daddy does." "Blain, why do you want to wear a belt buckle as big as your head?" Can you guess why? Why do you do what you do?

Follow God's example, therefore, as dearly loved children and walk in the way of love, just as Christ loved us and gave himself up for us as a fragrant offering and sacrifice to God. EPHESIANS 5:1,2

Look around your home and try to count the crosses that you have on the walls, shelves, or in a jewelry box. The cross is important to Christians because it reminds us that Jesus made a sacrifice to God the Father by dying for all of our sins. Right now you are God's dearly loved child because Jesus loves you!

How are you going to thank God for his love? As God's child, you are to do what God does. You are to imitate God, to follow his example. You can't send a thank you card to heaven, but you can show God that you are thankful by loving others. You can show God that you treasure the forgiveness he gives you by forgiving others. You can live and love because Jesus first loved you.

- What motivates you to serve Jesus and live a life of love?

- Make a plan of how you are going to show Jesus' love by being kind to someone today and tomorrow.

Ask God to help you love others like he has loved you.

Thanks Living

Remember to Say Thank You

❖

Did you remember to say thank you? Saying thanks shows that you consider the one who gave you something to be an important part of your life. Remember to say thank you to others and to your God!

As for me and my household, we will serve the LORD.
JOSHUA 24:15

Joshua was the leader who led the children of Israel into the Promised Land. As their leader, he reminded the people to be thankful for everything God had done. The Lord chose the nation of Israel to be his special people who would receive his Word and promises. God protected them against their enemies by parting the Red Sea and destroying Pharaoh's army. The reason the Israelites were now in the Promised Land was because God fought for them and gave the land to them as a gift. However, many Israelites were tempted to forget what God had done for them and, as a result, they were tempted to forget to say thank you.

Have you ever bragged about your grades, your abilities as an athlete, or how well you can do something? When you boast about yourself, you aren't being thankful for the gifts God has given you. You have forgotten that all your gifts and talents are from the Lord. Joshua reminded the Israelites to say thank you, not just through their prayers, but also through the way they lived their lives. Joshua was going to thank God by teaching his family to serve the Lord.

• Make a list of the things God has done for you today.

• How can your family thankfully serve the Lord over the next few days?

Ask God to give you a thankful heart and life for all that he has done for you.

Thanks Living

Thankful for Bad Days

❖

The devotion's title seems kind of strange, doesn't it? How can we be thankful when we have bad days and when nothing turns out right? Do we really have to be thankful for the rotten days?

God teaches that we can be thankful also for those days!

The royal administrators, prefects, satraps, advisers and governors have all agreed that the king should issue an edict and enforce the decree that anyone who prays to any god or human being during the next thirty days, except to you, Your Majesty, shall be thrown into the lions' den. Now when Daniel learned that the decree had been published, he went home to his upstairs room where the windows opened toward Jerusalem. Three times a day he got down on his knees and prayed, giving thanks to his God, just as he had done before. DANIEL 6:7,10

Daniel didn't go home to complain to God. Daniel didn't throw a temper tantrum or scream, "It's not fair." Daniel understood that he could be thrown into the lion's den if he worshiped the Lord. So what did he do? He went home in order to pray and give thanks to his God, just as he had done before! Daniel was thankful because he was able to take his problems to God. Daniel was in the habit of worshiping God and thanking him for being in control of even the bad days. The bad days give us opportunity to rely on God and turn to his promises.

- Talk about at least one good thing and one bad thing that happened to you today.

- What promise of God will help you handle the bad thing that happened?

Pray that the Lord gives you a thankful heart during challenging times.

Perfect Love

The Worst To-Do List Ever

❖

Have you ever had a to-do list at school or at home? What is the worst chore you have been asked to do? God's Word teaches that there is a chore Jesus has taken off our our spiritual to-do list.

On one occasion an expert in the law stood up to test Jesus. "Teacher," he asked, "what must I do to inherit eternal life?" "What is written in the Law?" he replied. "How do you read it?" He answered, " 'Love the Lord your God with all your heart and with all your soul and with all your strength and with all your mind'; and, 'Love your neighbor as yourself.' " "You have answered correctly," Jesus replied. "Do this and you will live." LUKE 10:25-28

An expert in God's law asked Jesus what we must do to have eternal life. Jesus answered that if a person perfectly loves God and his or her neighbor, the person will go to heaven. What's the problem? No one, not even an expert of the law, has loved perfectly all of the time. You are going to heaven, not because of the love you have for God and others, but because of the perfect love God has for you! Jesus did accomplish God's to-do list perfectly by loving his Father with all of his heart and by giving himself on the cross for every sinful neighbor who has ever lived. What must you do to inherit eternal life? It is not about what you can do, but it is what Jesus has done and the forgivingness he has given that gives you eternal life.

- No one can save himself. What message can you share with someone who is wondering what he has to do to be saved?

Pray that the Spirit focuses you on Jesus and the love he has for you.

Perfect Love

Be a Neighbor

❖

What is a neighbor? Who is your neighbor?

> **He asked Jesus, "And who is my neighbor?"**
> **In reply Jesus said: "A man was going down**
> **from Jerusalem to Jericho, when he was attacked**
> **by robbers. They stripped him of his clothes, beat him**
> **and went away, leaving him half dead.**
> **A priest happened to be going down the same road,**
> **and when he saw the man, he passed by on the other side.**
> **But a Samaritan, as he traveled, came where the man was;**
> **and when he saw him, he took pity on him.**
> **He went to him and bandaged his wounds,**
> **pouring on oil and wine. Then he put the man**
> **on his own donkey, brought him to an inn and**
> **took care of him. Which of these . . . do you think**
> **was a neighbor to the man who fell**
> **into the hands of robbers?" The expert in the law replied,**
> **"The one who had mercy on him." Jesus told him,**
> **"Go and do likewise."** LUKE 10:29-31,33,34,36,37

Jesus doesn't really teach us who our neighbors are, but he does teach us how to be a neighbor. God wants you to show love, care, and compassion to those who are in need. But why would you want to help others whom you don't even know? Jesus didn't just help you, he saved you by coming to your rescue. He willingly put himself in danger when he went to the cross and suffered your punishment for you. Jesus is the ultimate neighbor. Because of his extraordinary love, you can be a neighbor to others.

- Who are some people you are able to help? How are you able to help them?

Ask God to fill you with compassion for those who are in need.

Perfect Love

Jesus Loves You!

❖

Why do you do what you do as a Christian? Why do you love and show kindness to others? The reason you love isn't only because you love Jesus, but because he loves you.

We love because he first loved us. 1 JOHN 4:19

Can you pour water from an empty pitcher? No! First you have to fill up the pitcher so that you can fill up the glasses on the table. The same is true about your heart when it comes to loving God and others. The love that you have for others isn't perfect. Do you ever feel that you don't love someone, or that you don't have to love them because they were unkind to you? Go to Jesus' cross when you feel loveless and think about the love Christ has for you. Jesus' love is so great that he gave his life for you. Jesus loved you even though you weren't at the foot of the cross begging him to die for you. His loves spills into you and fills you up through the good news that you are forgiven for every mean act, every loveless word, and every time you didn't show love. Why do you do what you do? You live and love because Jesus loved you first!

- List Bible promises that show Jesus' love for you.

- How can Jesus' love spill out of your heart to others?

Thank God for the perfect love he gave you through his Son, Jesus.

Be Different

Looking Strange

❖

What does it mean to be proud? Pride causes people to think that they are better than others. If you think you are better than others, then you will start to think others don't deserve your love, your kindness, or your friendship. The world that doesn't believe in Jesus is filled with pride, but you who believe in Jesus are filled with his love.

**Live in harmony with one another.
Do not be proud, but be willing to associate
with people of low position.
Do not be conceited.** ROMANS 12:16

You like to dress a certain way. You talk and walk in your own distinct way. Being different isn't a bad thing. God has made everyone very unique. What is bad, however, is when you are tempted to be mean to someone who is different. Maybe someone doesn't look the same, talk the same, or smell the same as you or your friends. That doesn't give you the right to make fun of them or think you are better. Your Lord calls you to stand out from the world and maybe even look a little strange by loving those the world doesn't. Jesus wasn't too proud to save you. Your Savior loved you so much that he humbled himself to the point of dying for you on a cross. He forgives you for every time that you were too proud to help or play with someone. Jesus calls you his child, and he loves others through you!

- How might God bless you when you show love to those the world considers different?

- Who were some people that Jesus loved even though they seemed different or unlovable?

Ask God to love others through you.

Be Different

Love Even Your Enemies

❖

"She hit me first!" If someone hits you, does that give you the right to hit back? It is hard to be nice to someone who isn't very nice to you. Yet God wants you to be different from those who think that it is okay to hate your enemy.

You have heard that it was said, "Love your neighbor and hate your enemy." But I tell you, love your enemies and pray for those who persecute you, that you may be children of your Father in heaven. He causes his sun to rise on the evil and the good, and sends rain on the righteous and the unrighteous. MATTHEW 5:43-45

What? How could Jesus command you to love your enemies? Doesn't he know that they can be mean and hurtful? If they do something nasty first, why isn't it okay to do something back to them?

Who thinks like that? The sinful world does. The sinful nature loves to take revenge and get even with others. But you aren't a part of the world anymore. Through your baptism, the Holy Spirit separated you from the world. God loved you by sending his Son to free you from sin and showed amazing kindness by loving you when you were unlovable. God shows kindness to those who hate him and asks that you show love to those who hate you. Why should you? Loving your enemies is a powerful way to show that sin doesn't rule your heart—Jesus does.

- What is the only reason you are able to love your enemy?

- How did Jesus show love for his enemies? How does God show love to those who hate him?

Pray that the Spirit gives you strength to love your enemies.

Be Different

Forgive Them

❖

The Roman soldiers were feared because of their fighting style which featured short swords. Jesus didn't have a sword or armor, but he was true God. He had the power to call on thousands of angels to fight for him. Imagine how the mighty Roman soldiers would have hid from fighting angels! Jesus didn't call on his Father for angels to fight for him. He called on his Father for another reason.

Two other men, both criminals, were also led out with him to be executed. When they came to the place called the Skull, they crucified him there, along with the criminals— one on his right, the other on his left. Jesus said, "Father, forgive them, for they do not know what they are doing." And they divided up his clothes by casting lots. LUKE 23:32-34

Jesus didn't fight back or curse the soldiers for crucifying him. Instead, Jesus loved those who hated him. Jesus asked his Father to forgive the soldiers who didn't know him as the Son of God. Jesus didn't come to destroy sinners but to save sinners. Jesus wasn't fighting against soldiers—he fought for them. The Son of God gave up his life to forgive the sins of the world. Jesus was totally different from those who fight back, hold grudges, and hate others. He loved. He forgave. He saved. Jesus was different from the rest of the world so that he could forgive and save you! "Father forgive them." And he did—in Jesus.

- Why is it hard to forgive others?

- Jesus was perfect at forgiving. Because of Jesus' sacrifice, God sees you as perfect. How can you show thanks to God for forgiving you? Talk about what it means to forgive.

Ask God to empower you to forgive others.

God's Love for Me

Love That Chose Me

❖

The backyard kickball team and professional sports teams want the same thing—the best players. Usually the one who can kick the farthest, catch the best, or score the most points is the one who is picked first.

The Bible tells us that God chose you. Was it because God knew you would be the best Christian player on his team?

For [the Father] chose us in [Jesus] before the creation of the world to be holy and blameless in his sight. EPHESIANS 1:4

When did God choose you to be his? It was before he created the world. It was before clocks kept time. It was before the angels sang the Lord's praise. It was before you existed. God didn't choose you because you are more well-behaved than another boy or worked harder at home and school than the girl who lives down the road. God chose you before you could even do anything good for him. God chose you before you even lived and breathed. God chose you in Jesus not because you were sinless, but God the Father chose you to be holy and blameless in his sight! Think about it! In Jesus the sins you did yesterday and today are completely forgiven. Not even the devil can point his ugly finger at you and blame you for being guilty. In Jesus you are blameless because of the plan God had for you in eternity!

- What comfort do you have knowing God chose you from eternity?

- Explain who and what God sees when he looks at believers.

Praise God for knowing you before he created the world and for choosing you to be holy in Jesus.

God's Love for Me

Send Them My Love

❖

"Tell them hello from me!" "Send them my love!" Has anyone ever said that to you, or have you ever said that to anyone? We want others to know that we are thinking of them and that we love them.
How do we know that God loves us? He sent us his love!

This is how God showed his love among us:
He sent his one and only Son into the world that
we might live through him. This is love:
not that we loved God,
but that he loved us and sent his Son
as an atoning sacrifice for our sins. 1 JOHN 4:9,10

Grandma Gee-Gee sent her love to little Alex by sending him a birthday gift through Amazon. She loved her grandson so dearly and Alex loved his grandmother. Usually when we send our love to someone, we are confident that they love us in return. God showed us his love by sending Jesus into a world that didn't love him. You too were born dead in sin without love for God. That is why God sent us his Son, so that we would be cleansed from all our sin and live without guilt through Jesus. God sent Jesus so that we wouldn't be his enemies. Through faith we are his children who are united to him now and forever.

- List the blessings we have because God sent us his love.

- What are we motivated to do knowing God sent his Son into the world?

Place your sin before God and thank him for making you spiritually alive in Jesus.

God's Love for Me

Love Doesn't Hide

❖

What wouldn't you do if you wanted to keep your totally awesome, super fun, ultimate tree house all to yourself and a few friends? You wouldn't tell anyone about it!

God doesn't keep heaven a secret because he wants everyone to know about it, including you.

You also were included in Christ when you heard the message of truth, the gospel of your salvation. When you believed, you were marked in him with a seal, the promised Holy Spirit. EPHESIANS 1:13

Jimmy was so excited when Patty told him about the tree house she built behind her house. Not only did Patty tell him he could come over, but she also gave Jimmy the badge! Everyone who wore the badge was a part of the tree house club.

How did you get to be a part of God's family? It is because God doesn't keep the good news of Jesus a secret. The first time you heard that your sin was washed away might have been when you were baptized. Maybe you heard about Jesus from a friend who explained that the cross reminds us that Jesus died so we might live. The good news of Jesus doesn't make you a part of a tree house club, but it does make you a part of God's family. No, God doesn't give you a really cool badge that lets you into heaven. God gives himself to you! Through faith, the Holy Spirit lives in your heart and promises that God loves you now and will love you forever.

- Talk about the person or people God used to tell you about Jesus.

- Explain why you can be sure that you will be with God forever.

Thank God for making your heart the home where the Holy Spirit lives.

Live the Unexpected Life

The World Does It

❖

Making jello can be fun. After you add water to the powder and pour it into a mold, it takes on that shape. Your attitude can be like jello in the sense that it starts to look like the example we follow. What mold do others expect you to use?

Do not repay anyone evil for evil.
Be careful to do what is right in the eyes of everyone.
ROMANS 12:17

Have you ever pushed someone who pushed you? Did you ever say something nasty back to the person who made fun of you? Have you ever felt hate in your heart for someone who hurt you? The sinful world tells you that you can be evil to someone if he or she was evil to you first. The world says that, but the Lord doesn't. It is a sin to do wrong, say what is wrong, and think what is wrong, even if someone was nasty to you. Your heart and attitude isn't molded like jello to look like the world around you. Your heart is molded to look like Jesus. He didn't repay evil with evil, but conquered evil with his holy precious blood and his death on the cross. He forgave all of your mean actions and nasty words. Jesus' forgiveness is so powerful that he even cleanses the sinful thoughts from your heart. You no longer are like the world, but like Christ!

- There are going to be times when people say nasty things and do mean things to you. What can you do in return that pleases God?

- Should you care about the way others judge your actions and words? Why?

Pray that the Spirit uses the Word to mold you to be like Jesus.

67

Live the Unexpected Life

It Will Only Take One

❖

What is revenge? Should you pay someone back for the hurt he or she caused you?

> **David and Abishai went to the army by night, and there was Saul, lying asleep inside the camp with his spear stuck in the ground near his head. . . . Abishai said to David, "Today God has delivered your enemy into your hands. Now let me pin him to the ground with one thrust of my spear; I won't strike him twice." But David said to Abishai, "Don't destroy him! Who can lay a hand on the LORD's anointed and be guiltless?"** 1 SAMUEL 26:7-9

Abishai expected David to kill his enemy Saul. It only would take one swift thrust of Abishai's spear and David's enemy would be dead. But David understood that it wasn't his responsibility to pay Saul back for the times he had tried to kill David. God would deal with Saul in his own way and in his own time. It only would have taken one thrust of Abishai's spear to kill Saul, and it only takes one act of revenge to earn eternal death in hell for yourself. It can be very difficult to love those who are unlovable. But that is what Jesus did for you. You were God's enemy because of sin, and yet Jesus died for you. Jesus loved the unlovable by freeing you from the sin of hatred and revenge. Don't show your enemies what they expect, but show them the love of Jesus that will be completely unexpected.

- The devil always promises that you will feel better after revenge. What usually happens to your heart after taking revenge?

- How does the Lord's Prayer teach us to fight against revenge?

Pray for your enemies.

Live the Unexpected Life

What They Will Come to Expect

❖

People come to expect things after they experience it many times. If you turn the bathroom faucet on, what do you expect? If you flip the light switch on, what do you assume will happen? What do others expect from you?

Love must be sincere. ROMANS 12:9

What have your parents come to expect from you when you are asked to do your chores? What have your siblings or friends come to expect when they ask you for help? Are there times when people expect you to be cranky, grumpy, and crabby? Remember, being a crank is a choice that you make, and a sinful choice at that, because it doesn't show love. You shouldn't have to be bribed with a new toy or the promise of doing something fun before being respectful and obedient. Loving your family or friends only when they do something nice for you isn't sincere love. Your love hasn't always been sincere, but Jesus' love for you has. Jesus obeyed his Father perfectly and completed everything he was asked to do in order to save you. What did Jesus' mother and family expect from him? They came to expect perfect respect and a willing helping hand. There wasn't a day when Jesus chose to be cranky, crabby, and loveless. Love must be sincere—and Jesus' love is! Rejoice that your family and friends will experience Jesus' unexpected love and that they will experience it through you!

- What will sincere love look like in your home? At school? With your friends?

- It is vital to be filled up with love before love can spill out of you. How does Jesus daily fill you with his love?

Thank Jesus for his sincere and unfailing love for you.

Protecting the Fourth Commandment

Honor Your Authorities

❖

How are parents and those in authority blessings to you? What does it mean to honor your parents? Describe what dishonoring your authorities may look or sound like. The Lord gave you the Fourth Commandment so that you would protect the gift of parents and authorities.

Children, obey your parents in the Lord, for this is right. "Honor your father and mother"—which is the first commandment with a promise— "so that it may go well with you and that you may enjoy long life on the earth." EPHESIANS 6:1-3

To honor your authorities, especially your parents, means to think of them as valuable gifts that were given to you. Are moms and dads perfect? No, but God has chosen them to watch over you and be a blessing to you. God commands that you are to put your faith in action by showing love to the representatives he has placed in your life. Parents are God's representatives! If you dishonor your parents, you are dishonoring God. If you honor your authorities, you are respecting God and showing him that you are thankful for the love, care, and protection that he graciously gives. No, your parents aren't perfect, but you aren't either. That is why you have a perfect Jesus who forgives you and calls you his dear child through your baptism.

- The apostle Paul tells us that the Fourth Commandment is unique because it is the first commandment with a promise. Why does God attach a promise to this commandment?

- The greatest gift that we have is Jesus' forgiveness. This week consider forgiving each other by saying, "I forgive you and Jesus does too."

Thank God for the parents and grandparents he has placed in your life.

70

Protecting the Fourth Commandment

Perfect Obedience

❖

What do you think Jesus was like as a young boy growing up in Nazareth? What do you think it would have been like to be Mary and Joseph raising Jesus as their son? The Bible doesn't tell us much about Jesus' childhood, but we do know that he was obedient.

Then [Jesus] went down to Nazareth with them and was obedient to them. But his mother treasured all these things in her heart. And Jesus grew in wisdom and stature, and in favor with God and men. LUKE 2:51,52

What does it mean to be obedient? Yes, it does mean that you do what you are told to do, but being obedient is more than following the rules. Obedience isn't just about the action you do, but it is about the attitude you have. Dad and Mom are in your life to give you direction, guidance, and discipline. Jesus willingly and cheerfully placed himself under the authority of Joseph and Mary while he grew up in their home. Mary appreciated this and treasured her son. God too was pleased with Jesus' obedience and perfection, because through his perfect Son he would save you from the times you are disobedient, disrespectful, and have a sour attitude. Jesus was perfectly obedient for you, and his perfect obedience God credits to you through faith. Treasure that in your heart!

- What are some sour attitudes you need to repent of? What godly attitudes can you display that will bring joy to your parents?

- Jesus loves you so much that he was willing to place himself under the authority of Joseph and Mary. How can you show love to your parents and those in authority?

Thank Jesus for being perfectly obedient for you.

Protecting the Fourth Commandment

A Child's Job Is Never Done

❖

What do you hope to be when you grow up? The Little League player might dream about being in the Major League. The stick figure artist may dream about seeing her paintings hang in a gallery. The science student might dream about finding the cure for a disease. You are growing up and will find yourself moving on from one stage of life to another. Celebrate those steps as you move on to bigger and better things. Yet there is one job in life that God never wants you to stop doing or move beyond.

**Listen to your father, who gave you life,
and do not despise your mother when she is old.**
PROVERBS 23:22

When can you stop listening to your parents? When you are 18 or 21? When you move out of the house? God's Word tells you to continue to listen to your father and don't despise your mother when she is old. Why? God gave you the gift of life through your parents. Your father has lived many more years than you have, which means he has more experience and knowledge than you. Show him respect by listening to him even when you are old. God formed you in your mother's womb, and she cared for you as her baby. Your great privilege in life is to put your faith into action by honoring Dad and Mom. As a son or daughter, there is nothing bigger or better that God wants you to do.

- Name some things your dad or grandfather has taught you.

- List at least two things that you love about your mother or grandmother.

Pray that Jesus keeps our families safe and their hearts focused on him.

A Faithful King

God Has His Reasons

❖

Many have asked, "Why do bad things happen to good people?" Why? God doesn't always give you the answer. Hezekiah was a good king who teaches you what to do when bad things happen and bad news is heard.

In those days Hezekiah became ill and was at the point of death. The prophet Isaiah son of Amoz went to him and said, "This is what the LORD says: Put your house in order, because you are going to die; you will not recover."
Hezekiah turned his face to the wall and prayed to the LORD, "Remember, LORD, how I have walked before you faithfully and with wholehearted devotion and have done what is good in your eyes." And Hezekiah wept bitterly. 2 KINGS 20:1-3

This test wasn't for God but for Hezekiah. The king didn't just turn to the wall, but he turned to God in prayer. Why did Hezekiah do this? Hezekiah was accustomed to turning to God when life was good, and now when life was bad he knew where to go. God wants you to grow in faith in good times so that you trust in his promises during the bad times. Prayer isn't the last thing that Christians do if nothing else works. Prayer is the first thing God wants you to do. When you hear bad news or experience something awful, turn to the Lord who loves you. Trust that he hears and answers you.

- Why is it easy to forget God during the good times? Why is it difficult to remember God during the bad times?

- How can bad times be some of the best times for a Christian's faith?

Pray that God gives you the strength to turn to him in good times and bad.

A Faithful King

An Answer

❖

Do you ever have to wait for an answer? Maybe your mom or dad has said, "We'll have to wait and think about that." Have you ever taken a test at school and weren't very excited to get the test back to see your grade? King Hezekiah was told by God that he was going to die. He prayed to the Lord and got an answer right away.

**Before Isaiah had left the middle court,
the word of the LORD came to him:
"Go back and tell Hezekiah,
the leader of my people, 'This is what the LORD,
the God of your father David, says:
I have heard your prayer and seen your tears; I will heal you.
On the third day from now you will go up to the temple
of the LORD. I will add fifteen years to your life.
And I will deliver you and this city from the hand
of the king of Assyria. I will defend this city for my sake
and for the sake of my servant David.'"** 2 KINGS 20:4-6

King Hezekiah is a wonderful example of a faithful king, but it is the Lord who reveals himself as the true King of Judah. God listened to Hezekiah's cries and he answered. Not only did he promise that Hezekiah would live 15 more years, but he promised to protect the people of Judah. The child who was promised to be born from David's family would be the ruler of Israel. The Lord saved Hezekiah's life, and by preserving his chosen people, he was promising to save the world through Jesus. The Lord is your faithful King!

- What can you learn about your God through these Bible verses?

Ask God to strengthen your body and faith.

A Faithful King

A Sure Thing

❖

Hezekiah wanted to be sure that his life would be spared. God didn't sign a contract. The Lord didn't look Hezekiah in the eye and say, "I promise." The Lord did something only he could do.

**Isaiah answered, "This is the LORD's sign to you
that the Lord will do what he has promised:
Shall the shadow go forward ten steps,
or shall it go back ten steps?"
"It is a simple matter for the shadow to go forward ten steps,"
said Hezekiah. "Rather, have it go back ten steps."
Then the prophet Isaiah called upon the LORD,
and the LORD made the shadow go back the ten steps
it had gone down on the stairway of Ahaz.** 2 KINGS 20:9-11

At Hezekiah's time, they used sundials. The sun would shine on a pole and cast a shadow which would then tell what time it was. Hezekiah's life was at stake. The Lord wanted his king to know with certainty that he would live. It would be easy for the shadow to keep going forward as it always did, but to go backward would be impossible. God did the impossible! The Lord, who controls the shadows, showed Hezekiah that he was also in control of life and death. The Lord made a promise and kept his promise. Hezekiah lived.

- God doesn't promise you special signs. What does God give you so that you can be sure he loves and cares for you?

- What other miracles did God do in the Old Testament to assure his people of a promise?

Thank the Lord for his Word which assures us that he loves us and has our salvation in mind.

75

The Gift of Sleep

Rest Is Good

❖

What does it mean to have a good work ethic? If you have homework, don't do just enough to pass. If you are going to play sports, give it your best effort. Put the hours into playing your instrument if you want to be good someday. Hard work is good and God blesses you through it. But getting the rest that you need and taking a break as a family is also a blessing.

**In vain you rise early
and stay up late,
toiling for food to eat—
for he grants sleep to those he loves.** PSALM 127:2

This verse is talking to people who work hard raising crops and rarely take a break. Hard work is good, right? It isn't when people trust in hard work more than trusting in God to provide. Will the crop grow faster and taller if the farmer stands at the edge of the field and watches it grow? No. The Lord in his wisdom and love causes crops to grow and the fields to produce everything that entire countries need for food. It is foolish to work hard because you are worried if you are going to have enough. It is wise to work hard knowing that even when you sleep God is providing for you and blessing the work you did that day. Your work, sports, instrument, and chores will be there in the morning—and so will Jesus. Enjoy your rest tonight and rejoice in the gift of sleep.

- Why is it foolish to worry?

- God makes promises and blesses you. You are to work hard using your gifts and trusting in his promises. How will believing in these truths help you sleep?

Ask God to give you quiet, restful sleep.

The Gift of Sleep

Not Even a Quick Nap

❖

Do you ever take a nap? Sometimes when a person wakes up early or goes to bed too late, it just feels good to close your eyes for just a few minutes. Have you ever napped when you didn't want to? Some fall asleep during a movie or even nod off during school. It is hard to stay awake and pay attention when you are tired. Does the Lord ever take a nap?

**He will not let your foot slip—
he who watches over you will not slumber;
indeed, he who watches over Israel
will neither slumber nor sleep.**

**The LORD will keep you from all harm—
he will watch over your life;
the LORD will watch over your coming and going
both now and forevermore.** PSALM 121:3,4,7,8

Do you ever get scared at night when you are trying to sleep? What scares you? Maybe you are so busy worrying about the scary things you think might be there that you forget about the mighty God who is actually there. God watches over you. Your parents or grandparents may watch over you, but eventually they get sleepy too. God doesn't. He won't sleep or even take a ten-minute break. Why does he watch over you? Your Lord wants to protect you from all harm and to keep you safe with him. He will never stop watching over you in this life or in the next. So tonight sleep knowing that the Lord won't.

- God is even better than a nightlight. How is that true?

- What promises has God given you that shows he cares about your body and soul?

Ask God the Father to give you peace and happy dreams as you rest under his watchful care.

77

The Gift of Sleep

Personal Bodyguards

❖

Who usually has a bodyguard? The rich and powerful who need protection from crowds sometimes have bodyguards. The president of the United States has an army of bodyguards protecting him wherever he goes. How many bodyguards do you have? You have God's promise that you are guarded by the best.

**If you say, "The LORD is my refuge,"
and you make the Most High your dwelling,
no harm will overtake you,
no disaster will come near your tent.
For he will command his angels concerning you
to guard you in all your ways;
they will lift you up in their hands,
so that you will not strike your foot against a stone.** PSALM 91:9-12

God promises that whether you are awake or sleeping he is with you. Not only is the Lord watching over you, but he promises that his angels are also. Right now angels are carrying out the Lord's command to guard you. How would you feel if God allowed your eyes to see all of the angels that surrounded you right now? Like many people in the Bible, you might gasp in fright or fall to the ground. Yet the angels are not surrounding you to hurt you but to protect you. They are on your side.

- The angels serve Jesus and always do what he commands. How is that comforting to you when you are awake or asleep?

- Think of times in the Bible when angels appeared visibly. Can you describe what the angels looked like?

Thank God for being with you always and for sending his angels to guard you.

Certain in Jesus

Hope!

❖

How would you define hope? What are some things you hope for? You might hope for the one toy that you always wanted, but are you sure you are going to get it? You might hope for a good grade on the test, but after the test you aren't quite sure you did that well. You might hope for sandwiches but get nachos. How is the hope we have as Christians different?

May the God of hope fill you with all joy and peace as you trust in him, so that you may overflow with hope by the power of the Holy Spirit. ROMANS 15:13

There is nothing uncertain about God. When God makes a promise, he always keeps it. He promised Adam and Eve that if they ate the forbidden fruit they would die, and through their sin death entered the world. God didn't destroy Adam and Eve but gave them hope. He promised that a Savior would be born. Jesus was born in Bethlehem and you put your trust in him. Jesus' forgiveness removes your sin and creates peace between you and God. With sins forgiven, you have the joy of knowing you will be with Jesus forever in heaven. There is nothing uncertain about these promises. The Holy Spirit will continue to share them with you so that you overflow with certain hope.

- Can you think of Old Testament promises that gave God's people joy and peace as they hoped in the Savior to come?

- What are some promises of God that give your heart hope as a New Testament believer?

Ask God to forgive you for doubting his promises and then **thank** God for the blessing of certain hope.

Certain in Jesus

Whether You Like It or Not

❖

Can you think of any Old Testament promises that are read during the Christmas season? Think especially of a promise that shows how the Messiah would be different and unique? Isaiah tells you.

The Lord himself will give you a sign: The virgin will conceive and give birth to a son, and will call him Immanuel. ISAIAH 7:14

Isaiah was meeting with stubborn king Ahaz, who didn't believe in God's promises. When he needed help, instead of praying to the King of kings, Ahaz asked an unbelieving king for help. God promised Ahaz that he would be safe and would win the future battle against his enemies. Ahaz even received an invitation from God to ask for a sign. But unbelieving hearts don't want anything to do with God. Yet God gave him a sign whether he wanted one or not. The Lord promised that even though Ahaz was unfaithful, God would remain faithful by sending his Son through a humble virgin. To Ahaz who didn't believe, this sign was foolishness. But for those who do believe, this sign is a promise that was fulfilled when God was born to Mary. Immanuel came to earth so that he could live perfectly for us and die as payment for our sin. Ahaz didn't like the sign that was given to him. Praise God that you cherish this sign and believe that Jesus fulfilled it. You can be certain that someday you will be with God in heaven.

- Immanuel means "God with us." In what ways does Scripture teach that Jesus is with you?

- God was faithful even when Ahaz wasn't. How do you see God's faithfulness today in the world and in your life?

Praise God for sending his Son in such a miraculous way.

WEEK 27 DAY 3

Certain in Jesus

Jesus' Jobs

❖

What job has God given you to do? God asks us to do many things in life: Be a student, a good neighbor, a faithful citizen, a respectful child, and a responsible adult. What jobs did Jesus have when he came to earth?

**The Spirit of the Sovereign LORD is on me,
because the LORD has anointed me to proclaim good news
to the poor. He has sent me to bind up the brokenhearted,
to proclaim freedom for the captives and
release from darkness for the prisoners,
to proclaim the year of the LORD's favor and
the day of vengeance of our God, to comfort all who mourn,
and provide for those who grieve in Zion—
to bestow on them a crown of beauty instead of ashes,
the oil of joy instead of mourning, and
a garment of praise instead of a spirit of despair.
They will be called oaks of righteousness,
a planting of the LORD for the display of his splendor.**
ISAIAH 61:1-3

Christ was speaking through the pen of Isaiah. The Father sent his Son, who was full of the Spirit, to preach the good news of sins forgiven. The good news of Jesus makes you spiritually rich with the promise that every heavenly blessing is yours. This good news heals your heart by removing from you all of your guilt and failures. But God doesn't leave you empty. The Holy Spirit fills you with the perfection of Jesus and describes you as oaks of righteousness—trees that are strong and *beautiful*.

- What were the jobs Jesus had to do?

- Look through these verses again. What blessings does the good news of Jesus bring to your life?

Praise Jesus for being perfect at his job.

81

A Big Announcement

Heavenly Notifications

❖

Technology has given us the ability to receive many different notifications. What are some devices that notify you of upcoming events? Long before there was modern technology, there were still important notifications that people received of upcoming events.

**Then an angel of the Lord appeared to him,
standing at the right side of the altar of incense.
When Zechariah saw him, he was startled and
was gripped with fear. But the angel said to him:
"Do not be afraid, Zechariah; your prayer has been heard."**
LUKE 1:11-13

How would you react if an angel appeared to you while you were brushing your teeth? Would you scream, or would you be too afraid? Zechariah didn't do anything to bring the angel to him, and he wasn't about to try to shoo the angel away. Angels are holy beings created by God to serve him, and they serve by perfectly doing what God desires. Their perfection reminds us that we aren't perfect in the least. Yet the angel's words weren't terrifying: "Do not be afraid!" There is tremendous love in these words. Sinners should be afraid, but the angel tells Zechariah that there is no need for fear; God had heard and answered Zechariah's prayers. God doesn't want you to live in absolute terror of him; and because of Jesus, you don't have to. Trusting in Jesus as your Savior from sin, you have been clothed in Jesus' own holiness. God doesn't see you as a sinner, but as a son or daughter whose prayers he loves to hear and answer.

- Hebrews 1:14 says, "Are not all angels ministering spirits sent to serve those who will inherit salvation?" What is the main role of God's angels?

Thank God for taking away your sin and fear through Jesus.

A Big Announcement

A Child With a Plan

❖

What are your plans for the future? You might like to think far into the future and have plans for when you graduate high school or college. Maybe your plans only reach as far as this weekend. Or maybe you are someone who doesn't make a lot of plans but likes to fly by the seat of your pants. God has extraordinary plans; his plans are eternal and they include you.

"He [John] will bring back many of the people of Israel to the Lord their God. . . . to make ready a people prepared for the Lord." LUKE 1:16,17

Before John the Baptist was born, God had plans for his life. The Holy Spirit would prepare hearts through the message John would speak. John's message wasn't always a pleasant one because he pointed out people's failure to keep God's commandments. John did this to show others that they had a need for a Savior. Do you take medicine if you aren't sick? No. Do you need a Savior if you have no sin? No. Sinners don't always want to admit or even see that they have sin. John came to prepare hearts by preaching a message of repentance. You too need to recognize your sin so that you clearly understand your need for Jesus and are ready to hear the good news that Jesus forgives your sins. Just as John baptized sinners, God gives you baptism to wash away all your guilt, because you too are included in his eternal plans.

- Why is it comforting to know that God's plans are eternal and that they never fail?

- What plans does God have for you as a Christian?

- What will daily repentance look like in your life and home?

Pray for the Spirit to prepare your heart for Jesus.

A Big Announcement

Trust the One Who Speaks

❖

Has anyone ever told you a story that you felt couldn't be true? Have you ever seen something on the internet that you didn't think could be true, and you found out later that it wasn't? If something seems too good to be true, it probably is. That might be a good rule of thumb to follow when listening to the words of sinners, but it doesn't apply when you are listening to God.

Zechariah asked the angel, "How can I be sure of this?
I am an old man and my wife is well along in years."
The angel said to him, "I am Gabriel. I stand
in the presence of God, and I have been sent to speak
to you and to tell you this good news.
And now you will be silent and not able to speak
until the day this happens, because you did not believe
my words, which will come true at their appointed time."
LUKE 1:18-20

Zechariah's elderly wife would give birth to a son who would be known as John the Baptist. What did Zechariah do when the angel told him this good news? He didn't believe the message. He didn't believe the angel or God, who sent the angel. Having faith simply means taking God at his word. God does not lie. God doesn't stretch the truth or back out on a promise. Your Lord made a promise to send John to prepare the way for the Messiah, and God kept his promise for you.

- Zechariah lost the ability to speak during his wife's pregnancy. Why would this have been so difficult?

- Even though Zechariah didn't believe God's message, what was God going to do anyway? What does this teach us about God's faithfulness?

Pray for the Spirit to give you a heart that takes God at his word.

Who, Me?

How Can It Be?

❖

Who, me? When have you heard that question being asked? Some ask it to evade the truth that they did something wrong. "Who, me? I didn't steal the cookie from the cookie jar!" Mary asked a similar question, though she wasn't trying to get out of trouble. She was trying to understand how she could be so blessed.

**The angel said to her, "Do not be afraid, Mary;
you have found favor with God.
You will conceive and give birth to a son,
and you are to call him Jesus. "How will this be,"
Mary asked the angel, "since I am a virgin?"
The angel answered, "The Holy Spirit will come on you,
and the power of the Most High will overshadow you.
So the holy one to be born will be called the Son of God."**
LUKE 1:30,31,34,35

God's Son was going to be born! Who, me? This question must have jolted through Mary's mind. She was a young lady who had never lived with a husband. How could she have a child? The Holy Spirit would give her a child in her womb, not just to be Mary's Savior, but yours. The name Jesus means "he will save." God was born to save you from sin. Who, me? Yes, you! How can this be? It is because the Most High God loves you and shows you favor by giving to you forgiveness through his only Son.

- Why do you think God chose Mary to be the mother of his Son?

- God chose you to be his because of grace, the unconditional love that flows freely from him to you. How does this give you peace and joy?

Thank God for sending a Savior for you.

Who, Me?

Yes, You!

❖

What chores and tasks do you dread doing? Why don't you like them? When things take much mental effort, take a long time, or take a physical toll, individuals often don't like those tasks. God, however, asks his people to do some especially difficult things. Mary gives us a good example of how we are to serve.

"I am the Lord's servant," Mary answered. "May your word to me be fulfilled." Then the angel left her. LUKE 1:38

Mary was going to experience the power of God, who was going to miraculously give her a son. She was young and didn't live with Joseph as her husband. The child who grew inside her womb was true God—he would be the Savior of the world! What God asked her to do was very serious and, at the same time, an extraordinary honor. What would you have done after hearing the news? The Bible doesn't tell us that Mary ran away to hide. She didn't tell God that the task was too difficult and that he should choose someone else. Mary accepted God's will as her own. She recognized who she was, a servant loved by God and through whom God chose to work. God loves you too and has chosen your gifts and talents to do his work and will. Instead of running away from school work, house chores, or difficult tasks, meet them with the same attitude that Mary had. You are God's servant! Who, me? Yes, you!

- God asks his people to do challenging work. What are some difficult things God asks his people to do?

- Describe the attitude of someone who has a servant's heart.

Pray that God gives you a servant-like heart.

Who, Me?

Slow Down

❖

Has a teacher ever told you that you need to take your time on your work? Have you ever heard a lifeguard scold someone for running near the pool? Too often people are in a hurry. If you don't slow down, you might miss some problems on your work sheet or you might get injured. God wants you to slow down so that you are spiritually safe and you don't miss any of his blessings.

Mary treasured up all these things and pondered them in her heart. LUKE 2:19

The shepherds hurried to Bethlehem to find Mary and Joseph with baby Jesus. The shepherds were full of energy as they hurried to the stable in careful search of the child and as they left to tell everyone what they had heard and seen. Mary took a quieter approach. She first treasured what she had just experienced. She had given birth to the Savior and marveled at the unexpected visitors, who told her about angels rejoicing over her son. She took it all in and then she carefully thought through everything that had happened. Most likely you have heard the Christmas story before. You might even be able to rattle off the facts and recite large sections of the Bible. Awesome! But don't forget to slow down and think through everything you have memorized and know. Slow down and consider carefully who was placed in a manger and what Jesus means to you. Slow down and do some of your own pondering as you quietly consider the gift of Jesus.

- What keeps you from carefully thinking about the true meaning of Christmas?

- What from the Christmas lesson do you especially treasure?

Pray that God gives you quiet moments to ponder his love.

Get Ready

Heart Construction

❖

How do you know when it's summer time? If you live in the north, you can be sure it's summer when you see many orange cones and construction vehicles on the roads. How were people to know that the Messiah was near? God promised there would be construction projects taking place. No, there wouldn't be orange cones and pieces of large machinery moving asphalt. God wasn't talking about road construction but heart construction.

**As it is written in the book of the words of Isaiah the prophet:
"A voice of one calling in the wilderness,
'Prepare the way for the Lord, make straight paths for him.
Every valley shall be filled in, every mountain and
hill made low. The crooked roads shall become straight,
the rough ways smooth.
And all people will see God's salvation.'"** LUKE 3:4-6

In ancient times, people would prepare roads for the king's arrival by removing obstacles and smoothing out the rough spots. For this project God sent a one-man crew! God wasn't interested in moving piles of dirt. God was interested in moving hearts; the tool that he used was his powerful Word. The Holy Spirit prepared hearts by John the Baptist's preaching of repentance. The law of God shows that everyone has failed to live up to God's perfect standard. This truth causes sorrow over sin and shows the need you have for a Savior. But God doesn't want you to see only your need, he wants you to see that Jesus fulfills your need by giving you salvation.

- Why is it necessary to repent every day?

- Will living in repentance be a happy or sad life? Why?

Ask God to fill your heart with the joy of salvation through the forgiveness of sins.

Get Ready

The Names Say It All

❖

Why is the naming of a child an important task? God promised to bring joy into the world through a baby, but this child wouldn't be an ordinary baby; nor would he have ordinary names.

**To us a child is born, to us a son is given, and
the government will be on his shoulders.
And he will be called Wonderful Counselor, Mighty God,
Everlasting Father, Prince of Peace.
Of the greatness of his government and peace
there will be no end. He will reign on David's throne
and over his kingdom, establishing and
upholding it with justice and righteousness
from that time on and forever.
The zeal of the LORD Almighty will accomplish this.** ISAIAH 9:6,7.

Jesus grew up in a carpenter's home, but he was God's Son. His names say it all about what he would do. Jesus is Wonderful Counselor by speaking the truth. Jesus showed he is Mighty God by the miracles he did. The good news of forgiveness creates faith in hearts; in this way Jesus makes you his children and is the Ever-lasting Father who cares for you. Jesus gave up his life to cancel the debt of sin and satisfy God the Father's wrath once and for all. The Father raised Jesus to life on the third day to publicly proclaim him to be his Son, the Prince of Peace. Jesus' names say it all; and what he does, he does for you!

- What promises in this passage give you the confidence that God could do—and did—wonderful things for sinners?

- How did Jesus show himself to be Mighty God when he lived on earth?

Ask God to fill your heart with peace.

Get Ready

Ready?

❖

Are you ready? A dad might say those words before he tosses the ball to his daughter. Mom might ask the question before she lets the swing go. These words are spoken so that you know what is coming and you can be prepared. But how do you feel when you don't know what is about to happen and you get surprised?

There were shepherds living out in the fields nearby, keeping watch over their flocks at night. An angel of the Lord appeared to them, and the glory of the Lord shone around them, and they were terrified. But the angel said to them, "Do not be afraid. I bring you good news that will cause great joy for all the people. Today in the town of David a Savior has been born to you; he is the Messiah, the Lord." LUKE 2:8-11

Brighter than a flashlight, the glory of the Lord shown around the terrified shepherds, but merciful words were spoken to them, "Don't be afraid." The angel wasn't there to harm them. The angel was there to proclaim good news that would bring them joy—a message that still brings us joy today. When Jesus was born, the Father fulfilled his promise to send a Savior. There is no need to fear because you are forgiven. There is no need to be terrified of death because you are saved. Even though unexpected things do happen in life, you have something that will never change. You have Christ the Lord who brings you lasting joy.

- Why do you think God chose the shepherds to be the first ones to hear of Christ's birth?

- How does Jesus give you joy?

Pray that the Spirit removes your fear with his Word

Led by a Star

Remarkable Guests

❖

How do parents get the word out that their baby has been born? Mary didn't have to send texts, create an announcement card, or even phone a friend. God the Father was excited to share the news of his Son's birth and took care of the announcements. He used a star to bring remarkable visitors to Jesus.

**After Jesus was born in Bethlehem in Judea,
during the time of King Herod, Magi from the east
came to Jerusalem and asked,
"Where is the one who has been born king of the Jews?
We saw his star when it rose and have come to worship him."**
MATTHEW 2:1,2

The Bible doesn't mention the Magi's names, how many there were, or what they looked like. Why do you think that is? God knows that it is easy for us to get distracted from what is important. If the Bible gave all of the details about the Magi from the east, you might get so focused on the mysterious visitors and fail to focus on the One whom they visited. Why would the Magi travel so far and search so long? They knew an ordinary baby's birth isn't announced by a star! They believed that Jesus was the King of the Jews who came to be their Savior and the King of their hearts. The Magi had purpose, and so do you. Your purpose in life is to worship Jesus. Search for him, not by following a star, but reading the Word.

- What does it mean to worship? What are some distractions in life that tempt us to ignore worshiping Jesus?

- How are you able to worship Jesus daily in your home?

Praise God for sending his Son to be the Savior of all people.

Led by a Star

A Remarkable Search

❖

Think of something you once lost and had to search for. Did you look under the bed or in your closet? Did you have to clean out your locker or desk to find it? Where do you search when you want to find Jesus and the answers to your spiritual questions?

> **When [Herod] had called together all the**
> **people's chief priests and teachers of the law,**
> **he asked them where the Messiah was to be born.**
> **"In Bethlehem in Judea," they replied,**
> **"for this is what the prophet has written:**
> **" 'But you, Bethlehem, in the land of Judah,**
> **are by no means least among the rulers of Judah;**
> **for out of you will come a ruler**
> **who will shepherd my people Israel.' "** MATTHEW 2:4-6

Where did the pastors and teachers of the Jesus' day look to find the answers? They found the answer to where the promised king would be born in the Scriptures. When you have fears, doubts, and problems, where do you look for answers? Maybe you can't always say that you first look to the Bible. Is it because the Bible is too big? Is it because you doubt that you will find the answers? Could it be that sometimes you are too lazy? God does have the answers for our lives, and his Word always leads us to Jesus. The Savior was born in Bethlehem to be the Good Shepherd who would forgive your laziness and be the answer to your sins. Do you have God's Word? Then you have God's answers, the truth, and his forgiveness.

- What does the prophet say the Christ would be like?

- What are some questions the Bible answers for you?

Thank the Holy Spirit for speaking to you through the Word.

Led by a Star

Remarkable Gifts

❖

Name some gifts you have bought for friends and family members. Were these things they needed? Were these things they could play with and use? We give gifts based on what our friends like and what our families need. The Magi gave gifts to Jesus for a different reason.

**When they saw the star, they were overjoyed.
On coming to the house, they saw the child
with his mother Mary, and they bowed down
and worshiped him. Then they opened their treasures
and presented him with gifts of gold, frankincense and myrrh.**
MATTHEW 2:10,11

Most likely Jesus was only a very small child when the Magi visited. Would you want a baby playing with a bar of gold or a bag of coins? Most wouldn't give a fragrant sticky paste to a baby, but the Magi did. The Magi gave the very best that they could as an act of worship. When you go to church, the offering plate isn't passed around because God needs your money. No, God is the creator of the heavens and earth who doesn't need anything. You give to worship the Lord and praise Jesus for being born as the Savior of the world—as your Savior and greatest treasure!

- The Magi obviously had a plan to give gifts to Christ after they found him. How can planning your church offering help you give your very best to God?

- What are some of the things your offerings are used for? Is there a special project that you would like to give to at your church or school in order to worship Jesus?

Ask the Lord to bless you with a generous heart that is filled with praise for him.

The Wow Factor

Praising God for the Past

❖

What makes you say "Wow?" Is it a video that shows someone making an impossible basketball shot? Is it a beautiful sunset, as you marvel at God's amazing palette of color? As God's people, we are able to marvel at the world around us, but we are also able to marvel at what God reveals to us in his Word. The Bible gives us many reasons to say "Wow!"

I will tell of the kindnesses of the LORD, the deeds for which he is to be praised, according to all the Lord has done for us—yes, the many good things he has done for Israel, according to his compassion and many kindnesses. ISAIAH 63:7

Old Testament history reveals that so often Israel was unfaithful to God by breaking his commandments and even refusing to listen to his Word. How would you like it if every event of your life was written down for everyone to see or recorded for everyone to hear? Would it reveal that you were always faithful to God and perfect in every way? No, but it would reveal that God is faithful to every promise, and it would demonstrate his incredible kindness to you. God didn't destroy Israel because of their sin. Instead, he continued to care for Israel so that from them a Savior from sin would be born. And God shows you kindness by not condemning you to hell, but giving you Jesus, who forgives you, so that he can show you his kindness forever in heaven. Wow!

- List some things the Lord did in the Old Testament that cause you to praise him.

- What are some deeds that God did in your life that cause you to say "Wow"?

Thank God for showing you compassion and kindness.

The Wow Factor

The Good and the Bad

❖

Have you ever seen or experienced the power of water? Homes can be washed out into the ocean. A river can cut a new channel through the landscape. Have you ever heard the crack of thunder? Wow, that can be scary! God's Word tells us of good and bad things that may cause us to say "Wow."

When [the Magi] had gone, an angel of the Lord appeared to Joseph in a dream. "Get up," he said, "take the child and his mother and escape to Egypt. Stay there until I tell you, for Herod is going to search for the child to kill him." MATTHEW 2:13

The promised Messiah was born! The Magi searched for Jesus in order to worship the newborn King. However, not everyone was happy. King Herod hated the thought of another king. But of course, he was thinking of a different kind of king, so he wanted to search for the baby to kill him. Wow! You can't be accused of searching for Jesus in order to kill him, but are you guilty of searching for the wrong kind of king, or not eagerly searching for him at all? Have you ever grumbled because you didn't want to go to church? Maybe you didn't want to hear what God's Word says because you didn't want to be told you were doing something sinful. Why wasn't Herod able to kill Jesus? Jesus came to earth, not to be killed by Herod, but to freely give his life as a sacrifice that would make you his forgiven sons and daughters. The Father kept his Son safe to be your Savior and the King who rules your heart. Wow!

- How did God keep Jesus safe?

- What are ways that God keeps you safe both spiritually and physically?

Ask God to give you the desire to search his Word.

The Wow Factor

Perfect Timing

❖

Have you ever said something at the wrong time? Have you ever missed out on something fun because you were just too late? God the Father has perfect timing and he never misses an opportunity to bless you.

**When the set time had fully come, God sent his Son,
born of a woman, born under the law,
to redeem those under law,
that we might receive adoption to sonship.** GALATIANS 4:4,5

What do you need to have in order to go to heaven and live with God forever? Perfection! You know from experience that no one is perfect in what they think, say, or do. No one, that is, except Jesus. God sent his Son to do what you and I cannot do—live a perfect life under the law. When Jesus grew and the time was right, he gave himself as a perfect sacrifice on the cross to buy you back from sin, death, and the devil.

If you pay for a pack of gum at the store, to whom does it belong? It belongs to you. Christ paid for you and you are his! Satan cannot accuse you anymore and death will not be able to hold you. When the Father looks at you, he sees Jesus' holiness! Through faith you are an heir of God who has received every spiritual blessing that God has to offer, all because of God's perfect timing when he sent his Son for you. Wow!

- What is an heir? What are some spiritual blessings that are yours as spiritual heirs through faith in Jesus?

- What are two reasons that Jesus was born as true man in order to save you?

Thank the Father for having perfect timing and sending you the perfect Savior.

Jesus for Me

The Right Thing to Do

❖

Why do people need to be baptized? For the same reason that it is so important to go to church and be in the Word, you need forgiveness through the good news of Jesus. Why did Jesus need to be baptized? He wasn't baptized because he had sin, but because he had love.

**Then Jesus came from Galilee to the Jordan
to be baptized by John. But John tried to deter him,
saying, "I need to be baptized by you,
and do you come to me?"
Jesus replied, "Let it be so now; it is proper for us
to do this to fulfill all righteousness."
Then John consented.** MATTHEW 3:13-15

John couldn't give anything to Jesus, but he needed what only Jesus could give to him. Jesus knew God the Father sent him to give the world the forgiveness that was needed, and that is why he insisted on being baptized. First, Jesus' love for the Father moved him to do what the Father wanted, and what the Father wanted was to have the Son baptized. Second, Jesus' love for you was so immense that he was baptized for you. Jesus had no sin, but you do, and when Jesus was baptized, he was giving himself as your substitute. Jesus was willing to live the perfect life you needed. Jesus was willing to be punished for your sin on the cross. You need Jesus, and Jesus willingly gave himself to you at his baptism. You have a right relationship with God because Jesus fulfilled all righteousness for you.

• What does it mean that Jesus is your substitute?

Thank the Father for giving you his Son as a substitute who lived and died for you.

97

Jesus for Me

Clearly Marked

❖

What mark would you expect to find on a pirate's treasure map? Start digging where an X marks the spot! Underneath the X is the promise of treasure and wealth! However, a boatload of treasure won't save you and a chest filled with gold doesn't wash away your sin. You need the Savior God promised long ago, and God made sure that he was clearly marked.

Then John gave this testimony:
"I saw the Spirit come down from heaven as a dove
and remain on him. And I myself did not know him,
but the one who sent me to baptize with water told me,
'The man on whom you see the Spirit come down and
remain is the one who will baptize with the Holy Spirit.'
I have seen and I testify that this is God's Chosen One."
JOHN 1:32-34

The Savior doesn't wear an X on his chest, but he has been clearly marked. After Jesus' baptism, the Holy Spirit came down as a dove to reveal to John the Baptist that Jesus was chosen to save the world from sin. There is no need to search in order to find out who the Savior is. There is no need to wonder how you will repair your relationship with God. There is no need to get a pirate's treasure map in hopes you can unearth spiritual wealth. The Spirit made it clear that the search is over because Jesus is the Son of God who came to save you. Jesus is your greatest treasure.

- After God revealed to John who Jesus was, what did John do?

- To whom can you reveal Jesus as the Savior and Son of God?

Ask God to give you courage and the words to share Jesus with others.

Jesus for Me

There He Is!

❖

Why is it hard to keep good news to yourself? What good news have you shared with others lately? After God the Father revealed through Jesus' baptism that he was the Christ, John the Baptist couldn't help but proclaim the good news. The good news John shared wasn't just exciting or encouraging: The good news of Jesus is lifesaving!

The next day John saw Jesus coming toward him and said, "Look, the Lamb of God, who takes away the sin of the world!" JOHN 1:29

John knew who Jesus was so he pointed out Jesus to others by telling them to look. You know who Jesus is, but do you sometimes fail to look to him as the Lamb of God who takes away sin? Instead of living in his forgiveness, do you ever keep the pit of guilt in your stomach? Have you ever worried about whether you were going to heaven? When you have feelings of guilt and fear, listen to what John says, "Look, the Lamb of God, who takes away the sin of the world!" You are included in the word *world*. Jesus loved you so much that he willingly became the sacrifice that freed you from guilt and now is the Savior who removes all of your fears. You are saved through the Lamb of God and are eternally safe with Jesus. Look, the Lamb of God, who took away all *your* sin!

- John the Baptist couldn't keep the good news to himself. What is the most important good news that people need to hear?

- What are ways you and your church can point people to look at the Lamb of God?

Thank God for anyone who points you to look at Jesus.

Did You See That?

The Hope of Friends

❖

Have you ever had a friend who was really sick or hurt? How did you feel? What did you do? Perhaps, to give encouragement, you could share your own personal stories of how a doctor helped you. If a friend was on crutches, you could help her carry her books to class or hold the door for her. However, when a friend is hurt, don't only focus on what you can do for him but focus also on whom you can share with him.

Some men came, bringing to him a paralyzed man, carried by four of them. Since they could not get him to Jesus because of the crowd, they made an opening in the roof above Jesus by digging through it and then lowered the mat the man was lying on. MARK 2:3,4

The friends worked hard to get the paralyzed man to the top of the house. Imagine what it must have looked like to Jesus when they began to dig through the roof! Why did they go through all of the trouble and hard work? They wanted to get their friend to Jesus. Many must have pointed to the ceiling and asked, "Do you see that?" Just imagine how the man's heart must have felt when the eyes in his paralyzed body could look upon the Lord, all because his friends put their hope in Jesus. Bringing soup to a sick friend is good. Visiting someone in the hospital is wonderful. But as a Christian the greatest gift you can share and give is Jesus.

- How could you share Jesus with a friend the next time he or she is sick?

- What are some Bible promises you could write in a get well card?

Ask God to heal those who are sick or hurt.

Did You See That?

The Forgiveness of a Savior

❖

No one likes to be sick or enjoys being injured. When you get a cold, you want it to go away immediately. When you want to play in the big game, but the doctor said you can't because of your injury, you feel sad. But Jesus teaches that being sick or injured isn't your biggest concern.

When Jesus saw their faith, he said to the paralyzed man, "Son, your sins are forgiven." MARK 2:5

The paralyzed man was lying on his mat in front of Jesus because he couldn't move his body. Did Jesus heal him immediately? No, not physically, but he did heal him spiritually. Jesus forgave the man all his sins. Having his sins forgiven didn't allow the man to skip and gallop down the streets, but it did promise him that he would walk the streets of heaven. Injury and sickness are reminders that there is sin in the world and that you are a sinner. Perfect health doesn't guarantee that you will live forever, and just because you are injury free doesn't mean that you can run through the gates of heaven. Jesus knew what the man needed. Jesus knows you need his forgiveness more than anything, and Jesus' forgiveness is what you have through faith in him! On this side of heaven you will be injured and will find yourself fighting sickness, but with your sins forgiven you will find yourself in heaven one day with Jesus.

- You aren't always going to be happy when you are sick or hurt, but you can always be filled with joy. Why?

- How can you daily hear or remember that your sins are forgiven?

Thank God for forgiving all sin and washing away all guilt.

Did You See That?

The Amazement of the Crowd

❖

Have you ever watched something amazing over and over? When an incredible athletic play or heroic act takes place, the video of the event may go viral. The crowds who gathered around Jesus saw something amazing. Christians can be thankful that long before the internet Jesus' miracles went viral.

"I want you to know that the Son of Man has authority on earth to forgive sins." So he said to the man, "I tell you, get up, take your mat and go home." He got up, took his mat and walked out in full view of them all. This amazed everyone and they praised God, saying, "We have never seen anything like this!" MARK 2:10-12

Why did Jesus do miracles? His miracles showed he loved people and wanted to help them. Miracles also, and most importantly, supported the message that Jesus preached. Jesus' miracles show that he didn't just talk about forgiveness, but he had the authority to forgive sins. Jesus did things only God could do because he is true God who lived on earth with flesh and bones. The man Jesus healed wasn't trapped in his paralyzed body anymore, and when he went home that day he wasn't trapped in his sin either! The Bible lets you *watch* this amazing event over and over again so that you can continue to praise your Father in heaven for his amazing Son and your forgiving Savior.

- What do you think the crowd did when they went home? How are you able to let this lesson go viral?

- What are some ways technology is being used to spread the news that Jesus is true God?

Ask the Spirit to use you to spread the message of Jesus' love and forgiveness.

A Miraculous Meal

Unexpected Supper Guests

❖

Has anyone ever shown up at your house unexpectedly while your family was eating supper? If a friend or family member did show up, would you tell him to get lost and send him away hungry? Today we are going to see what Jesus did with unexpected guests?

So [Jesus and his disciples] went away by themselves in a boat to a solitary place. But many who saw them leaving recognized them and ran on foot from all the towns and got there ahead of them. When Jesus landed and saw a large crowd, he had compassion on them, because they were like sheep without a shepherd. So he began teaching them many things. MARK 6:32-34

Jesus wasn't annoyed that his plans with his disciples had to change. Jesus didn't angrily drive the people away. He saw the crowd and had compassion on them. The original Greek word has the sense that his guts churned inside of him. Society today would say that Jesus' heart went out to them. Jesus felt deep love for the crowd of people and fed them the best spiritual food that he could provide. The Shepherd of his sheep fed their souls with his life-giving Word. Jesus looks on you with compassion too. He doesn't let your soul starve. Jesus feeds you with the good news that he is your Savior who forgives and loves you. He will never drive you away. He lived so that you may be with him forever.

- How would you define compassion?

- How does Jesus show his compassion toward you?

- In what ways can you show compassion to someone in your life?

Thank Jesus for showing compassion and love by speaking to you through his Word.

A Miraculous Meal

An Unexpected Source

❖

Where do you usually get your food? Some people have gardens and chicken coops. Others go to the supermarkets and grocery stores. The disciples didn't know where their food was going to come from. There weren't fast food restaurants or food carts in the remote location where they were. Though the villages were far away, Jesus wasn't.

**His disciples came to him. "This is a remote place,"
they said, "and it's already very late. Send the people away
so that they can go to the surrounding countryside and
villages and buy themselves something to eat."
But he answered, "You give them something to eat."**
MARK 6:35-37

Why did Jesus tell his disciples to feed the crowd? He knew that the disciples couldn't provide the amount of food that was needed. Jesus wanted his disciples to understand that what they faced was impossible for them; they had a need that they couldn't fill. There are times when Jesus allows you to face what seems to be the impossible because he is teaching you to rely on him, who can do the impossible. Jesus was teaching his disciples to come to him with their concerns and needs. Jesus invites you to go to him for all of your needs and rely on him when situations seem to be impossible. The disciples didn't know where the food was going to come from, but Jesus did, and he knows how he will provide for you too.

- What causes you to worry? How does this lesson help you battle against the sin of worry?

- How has Jesus provided for your family in what seemed like an impossible situation?

Ask God to forgive your worry and give you confidence to rely on Jesus for everything.

A Miraculous Meal

An Unexpected Supper

❖

What is your favorite treat? Snacks are good, but it can be fun to get a snack that you didn't expect like ice cream, fresh cookies, or fresh fruit. The crowd who ran to meet Jesus came to him unprepared. They didn't pack a lunch or bring a snack. This gave Jesus the opportunity to provide the unexpected.

Then Jesus directed them to have all the people sit down in groups on the green grass. So they sat down in groups of hundreds and fifties. Taking the five loaves and the two fish and looking up to heaven, he gave thanks and broke the loaves. Then he gave them to his disciples to distribute to the people. He also divided the two fish among them all. They all ate and were satisfied, and the disciples picked up twelve basketfuls of broken pieces of bread and fish. The number of the men who had eaten was five thousand.
MARK 6:39-44

Neither the disciples nor the crowd knew where the needed food was going to come from. Jesus knew. First he gave thanks to his Father, then he distributed the miraculous supper. There will be times when you will be tempted to worry and fear the worst. Why do hearts worry? It is because the sinful nature doesn't expect that Jesus can help or provide what we need. Jesus proved that he has the power to help by feeding more than 5,000 men, plus women and children! Your God will help you. He especially wants you to know that he is the Son of God who takes care of your greatest spiritual need—forgiveness.

- Why do you think Jesus told us how many leftovers the disciples picked up?

- What truths from this miracle bring you comfort and confidence?

Thank Jesus for the blessings he has provided for your family and church.

105

What Jesus Does

Jesus Watches

❖

"Hey, watch me!" It feels good when someone watches you and pays attention to what you are doing. It is also very comforting if someone is watching over you during scary situations. Mom or Dad might comfort you at night when it is dark. Walking with a friend instead of by yourself might help you feel more comfortable and not so alone. Jesus wants you to be confident that he watches over you. Even if you can't see Jesus, he sees you.

Later that night, the boat was in the middle of the lake, and he was alone on land. He saw the disciples straining at the oars, because the wind was against them. MARK 6:47,48

All night the disciples were straining at the oars. How do you feel when you are struggling? Do you ever feel like you are alone and the only one who is having a hard time? Maybe, like the disciples, you just feel tired and wonder where God's help is? Where was God when the disciples were straining at the oars? He was standing on shore watching his disciples. It was early in the morning when it would be difficult to see. As true God, Jesus had his eyes on those he loved. He was concerned for them. Jesus is concerned for you too. He loves you, and even if you can't see him, he is watching over you. Jesus did this for his disciples and he does this for you.

- How does knowing that Jesus watches over you during scary situations bring you comfort?

- Jesus did let his disciples struggle. Why does God let his people struggle?

Pray that the Spirit would give you confidence to trust that Jesus watches over you at all times.

What Jesus Does

Jesus Comforts

❖

What one thing makes you feel safe? There are many things people rely on to protect themselves in order to feel safe. But what do you do when there isn't a lock you can hide behind? What can you do when you can't run away from what is frightening? You can listen to Jesus who brings you incredible promises of comfort.

When the disciples saw [Jesus] walking on the lake, they were terrified. "It's a ghost," they said, and cried out in fear. But Jesus immediately said to them: "Take courage! It is I. Don't be afraid." MATTHEW 14:26,27

What could it be? The disciples thought that it had to be a ghost and screamed out in fear. How did Jesus remove their fear? Jesus had the disciples focus on him. "Take courage! *It is I.* Don't be afraid." What are you usually focused on when you are scared? You probably are thinking about the scary thing or imagining that the worst thing in the world could happen to you. When you do that, you are sinning by worrying and forgetting about your Jesus. Jesus is your Savior who loves you and who can walk on water! Jesus is the true God who tells you to be courageous because he is with you. Be courageous—you have Jesus. Don't be afraid—Jesus has you.

- Imagine you were a wave. What would you be thinking when Jesus was walking on you?

- Jesus doesn't always tell you what he is going to do. He simply says, "It is I. Don't be afraid." How can remembering these words bring you comfort when it comes to the unknown future?

Thank Jesus for chasing away your fears.

What Jesus Does

Jesus Rescues

❖

When can you walk on water? Only when the water is frozen. Peter was able to walk on unfrozen water because Jesus promised he could.

Then Peter got down out of the boat, walked on the water and came toward Jesus. But when he saw the wind, he was afraid and, beginning to sink, cried out, "Lord, save me!"

Immediately Jesus reached out his hand and caught him. "You of little faith," he said, "why did you doubt?"
MATTHEW 14:29-31

Peter's physical eyes and the eyes of his heart were focused on Jesus. Jesus was giving him the ability to do the impossible! But Peter saw the wind and the waves; he no longer focused on Jesus. He let go of the promise that Jesus would keep him from sinking. Down into the water Peter went. Jesus scolded Peter for not trusting. Should Jesus scold you? Have there been days where you worried whether everything would be okay? Have you even wondered if Jesus forgives you because you felt like you were sinking into an ocean of guilt? Oh, you of little faith. Trust in the Jesus who walked on the water and can do the impossible in your life. Believe that the Jesus who pulled Peter out of the water is the same Jesus who pulls you out of the pit of hell and guilt. You are rescued by Jesus. There is no need to be afraid.

- What are some blessings you give up if you don't trust in Jesus' promises?

- Jesus wasn't scared, even with the wind and the waves. How does Jesus' perfection bring you comfort and rescue?

Ask the Holy Spirit to keep your faith strong through the good news of Jesus.

The Most Important

An Honored Guest

❖

Things at your home would probably become very busy if you knew that Jesus was going to stop by. What would you need to do before he visited? What would Jesus want you to do during his visit?

**As Jesus and his disciples were on their way,
he came to a village where a woman named Martha
opened her home to him. She had a sister called Mary,
who sat at the Lord's feet listening to what he said.
But Martha was distracted by all the preparations
that had to be made. She came to him and asked,
"Lord, don't you care that my sister has left me
to do the work by myself?
Tell her to help me!"** LUKE 10:38-40

Martha was doing a good thing when she served Jesus. She, however, became so overwhelmed and distracted by what she wanted to give to Jesus that she forgot about what Jesus came to give to her. She thought that Mary was being lazy, which caused her to ask, "Lord, don't you care?" Do you ever feel overwhelmed with school, family, and all of the things that you need to do? Could it be that you even wonder sometimes if the Lord cares? The fact that God was sitting in Martha's house showed that he cared. The Son of God cared so much that he came to earth to be the good news of salvation. Jesus cares! Your greatest priority in life is not what you can give Jesus, but what Jesus has and can give to you.

- The most important reason why you go to church is to receive. Think through the church service and list all that you are given.

Thank God for ears that hear and a heart that believes.

The Most Important

Listen and Learn

❖

If you don't listen, you can't learn. What are some things that keep you from listening? At times it is hard to listen because you think you know what is best for you when you really don't.

"Martha, Martha," the Lord answered, "you are worried and upset about many things, but few things are needed—or indeed only one. Mary has chosen what is better, and it will not be taken away from her." LUKE 10:41,42

Have you been more of a Martha or more of a Mary lately? It is easy to become distracted and frustrated when your family's schedule becomes packed with so many good things that it turns into a bad thing because there is no room for Jesus. Martha needed to listen and learn that she was sinning by worrying about everything she needed to do instead of focusing on her Savior. Mary chose the one thing that was needed. She chose Jesus and her heart wasn't upset or worried. When you listen to Jesus, his promises give your heart the peace of forgiveness. Jesus gives you comfort by promising that you will never be taken from him. Only Jesus is needed, and through the Word, Jesus is given to you. Listen to him and learn of his amazing love.

- Life can become very busy. How can you, as a family, keep Jesus' word in your life even when things get hectic?

- To what can you say no so that you can say yes to listening to Jesus?

Pray that the Spirit gives you strength to make listening to Jesus a priority.

The Most Important

I Love It!

❖

How does someone show that he or she loves something? He might wear the shirt or hat that he loves every day. She might lock up her favorite piece of jewelry in a safe so that it won't get stolen or lost. When you love something, you will protect it and want it near you most, if not all, of the time. God's people feel the same way about his Word.

Oh, how I love your law! I meditate on it all day long.
PSALM 119:97

Did you hear the excitement of the psalm writer? He loves the law of the Lord, which means his heart is attached to God's law and gospel. God's people delight that the Lord guides them in life and gives direction through his Word. How awesome it is to know what God wants and that he gives you his law to protect you! However, God's law doesn't save you. The good news of a Savior from sin does! The gospel shows you the love that was so great, that God's Son would die so that you can live. Every day you wear the beautiful robe of Jesus' holiness and can treasure deep within your heart the promise that you are forgiven! Keep God's Word close to you and throughout your day think about the beautiful promises he gives to you.

- What does meditate mean? Make a plan that helps you and your family meditate on God's Word.

- Consider using your catechism and hymnal to help you think about God's Word. How might books like this help you meditate?

Ask God to give you a heart and mind that concentrate on his Word.

Christians Pray

God Always Hears

❖

How do you feel when your friends don't listen to you? How would you feel if Mom or Dad didn't listen when you badly needed their help? You might feel scared or lost, or maybe even find yourself in a dangerous situation. Does God ever ignore you? Will God ever fail to hear when you ask for help? Listen to what God has to say before you speak your next prayer.

I write these things to you who believe in the name of the Son of God so that you may know that you have eternal life. This is the confidence we have in approaching God: that if we ask anything according to his will, he hears us. And if we know that he hears us—whatever we ask— we know that we have what we asked of him. 1 JOHN 5:13-15.

The Holy Spirit is speaking to you who trust in Jesus' forgiveness and the promise of eternal life. Someday you will see Jesus with your own eyes, hear him with your own ears, and speak to him with your own mouth! But you don't have to wait to speak to Jesus. You are invited and commanded to boldly go to God in prayer. God will never ignore you but even promises that he will hear and always answer you. Remember God's promises and never stop praying!

- In his Word, God teaches what he wants you to pray for. If you want a strong prayer life, what is the first thing you need to do?

- God will always hear you! What are some specific things you can daily take to the Lord in prayer?

Pray for a heart that listens to God's Word and prays according to his will.

Christians Pray

The Ingredients of Prayer

❖

What is your favorite cookie? The right ingredients need to be used to get the tasty treat that you want. You don't bake cookies for Jesus, but you do put something together that pleases him. Today we hear God give directions about the ingredients that he urges us to put into our prayers.

I urge, then, first of all, that petitions, prayers, intercession and thanksgiving be made for all people—for kings and all those in authority, that we may live peaceful and quiet lives in all godliness and holiness. 1 TIMOTHY 2:1,2

What four different ingredients does the Holy Spirit teach you to include as you talk to God? The Father wants you to offer petitions or requests, that is, he wants you to list your needs. He cares for you and is delighted to provide for you. Even though you might not have anything specific on your mind, God wants you to talk to him. He wants you to simply share with him your ups and downs. Not only does he want to hear about your needs and concerns, but God wants you to pray about others also. You might pray for your family and friends, but don't forget your president and leaders. They have big jobs to do and need the help of your powerful God. Finally, praise God for everything that he gives to you. Thank him for the prayers that he has answered and for the blessings that he provides even without your asking. Think about these ingredients when praying and mix up some prayers for your Lord.

- How can remembering these four ingredients help you pray?

- What can you pray for when it comes to the president and your authorities?

Thank the Lord for the freedom you possess to publicly worship and pray.

Christians Pray

Lessons on Prayer

❖

If you could teach someone to pray, what would you teach him or her? Jesus teaches Christians some things to do and not to do when praying.

When you pray, go into your room, close the door and pray to your Father, who is unseen. Then your Father, who sees what is done in secret, will reward you. And when you pray, do not keep on babbling like pagans, for they think they will be heard because of their many words. Do not be like them, for your Father knows what you need before you ask him. MATTHEW 6:6-8

Have you ever kept calling someone's name hoping to get his or her attention? People think that if they keep calling, "Teacher, teacher," she will eventually answer. You don't have to raise your voice or pump your hand up and down to get God's attention. Your Father sees and hears you at all times. The first time that you speak words from your heart your Father hears them. God doesn't hear your prayers because you continue to repeat what you need over and over again. He doesn't answer you because you annoy him enough or become such a bother that he can't ignore you anymore. Your Father answers because you are his child who has been forgiven by Jesus. You are the child God the Father loves to care for and to provide for. Talk to God because he is always listening for you.

- Why can it be difficult to say long prayers? Why can short prayers be helpful?

- How would you answer someone who asked you how to pray?

Ask the Spirit to give you focus when praying.

Jesus Blesses Children

What Makes Jesus Angry?

❖

What do you think Jesus looks like? Do you picture him with an angry face? Maybe you don't want to think of an angry Jesus, but he was true man and had emotions just like you do. Yes, he did get angry, and the Bible tells us why.

**People were bringing little children to Jesus
for him to place his hands on them,
but the disciples rebuked them.
When Jesus saw this, he was indignant.** MARK 10:13,14

Why would the disciples stop the children from going to Jesus? They may have thought he was too busy or too tired. Maybe they thought that the children were going to bother Jesus or that he was too important to take time for little kids. Jesus was very important! However, though he is true God, he showed us that he still wants to be with children. Jesus came to this world to save both adults and children. Children and infants are sinners who need Jesus as their forgiving Savior. The disciples were keeping the ones Jesus loved from him, and he was angry about it. Praise God that you haven't been kept from Jesus. Thank your parents or grandparents who brought you to Jesus at your baptism. Be thankful for family devotions and that your family takes you to church. When you are in the Word, Jesus touches your heart with his love and promises. Jesus smiles when you are with him in his Word and blesses you through it!

- What are some of the ways your church brings children to Jesus?

- The parents brought the children to Jesus. How have your parents made sure that you grow up knowing Jesus as your Savior?

Thank Jesus for wanting to be with you now and forever.

Jesus Blesses Children

Come One and *Small*

❖

You usually have to be a certain height to ride on some rollercoasters at amusement parks. What a bummer it is when you are too young, too short, or not heavy enough! Being told that you just need to wait isn't very fun. You don't need to wait to experience the thrill of Jesus' love and the blessing of his forgiveness. Jesus calls out from the Bible for one and small to come to him.

[Jesus] said to them, "Let the little children come to me, and do not hinder them, for the kingdom of God belongs to such as these. Truly I tell you, anyone who will not receive the kingdom of God like a little child will never enter it." MARK 10:14,15

Jesus didn't only come for people 18 years and older. He didn't come just for those who were five feet tall or taller. Jesus loves the world. Jesus called the little children to him so that he could bless them and rule in their hearts through the Word he would speak to them. Jesus didn't point to his disciples as examples of faith. Jesus pointed to the children! Children trust that their parents will love them and care for them. The Spirit gives you a childlike faith that simply trusts that Jesus loves you and will care for you forever.

- How are children stopped from going to Jesus today?

- What are some truths that you believe, which show that the Holy Spirit has given you a childlike faith?

Pray for Christian families who read and study the Word of God together.

Jesus Blesses Children

In Jesus' Arms

❖

Are you a hugger? Jesus was.

**He took the children in his arms,
put his hands on them and blessed them.** MARK 10:16

As true God, Jesus came to earth and became a child himself. He grew up with his mother Mary, who held him and hugged him. We marvel at what we see in the Bible: Jesus scooped up sinful children and held them close to himself. Hugs aren't just for anyone. Hugs are given to the people you love and who are close to you. What was Jesus teaching his disciples? He loves children. Jesus loves you! Jesus put his hands on the children and gave them his blessing. Jesus put his blessing on you through your baptism. Every time you hear the Word it's as if Jesus is putting his hand on you as he gives you his promises. No, you don't get to sit on Jesus' knee and feel the warmth of his touch today, but you will when you go to heaven. The hands that were pierced with nails are the hands that will hug you, hold you, and wipe every tear from your eyes. How blessed you are to be forgiven, to be loved, and to know that you rest in Jesus' almighty arms!

- List the blessings you receive in church. What comfort do those blessings give you?

- What do you learn about Jesus as you see him taking the children in his arms? What confidence does this give you to go to Jesus through the Word and in prayer?

Ask Jesus to bless you both physically and spiritually.

A Glorious Glimpse

A Stunning Change

❖

Think of some occasions when you dress in your very best. Has anyone ever expressed surprise at how nice you look when you wash off the dirt and put on clean clothes? The disciples certainly were surprised at Jesus, not because he put on clean clothes, but that his entire appearance changed.

After six days Jesus took with him Peter, James and John the brother of James, and led them up a high mountain by themselves. There he was transfigured before them. His face shone like the sun, and his clothes became as white as the light. MATTHEW 17:1,2

Jesus walked on water. He raised the dead. He fed over 5,000 people at one time and calmed the sea. However, the Scriptures never tell us that Jesus was shining in bright glory when doing those miracles. He looked like other ordinary people who lived at that time. Jesus didn't look so ordinary on the mountain with the disciples when his glory was beaming brightly. The disciples would be able to tell others that even though Jesus walked, talked, and looked ordinary, he wasn't ordinary at all. Jesus knew that this special glimpse of his glory would be important for his disciples who would see him when he didn't look so glorious—on the cross. You aren't able to see Jesus' glory always shining brightly either, especially when life makes you sad or scared. That is why Jesus shows you a glimpse of his glory—so you can always trust that he is true God and your personal Savior.

- Think of other times when God allowed his glory to shine brightly for others to see.

- How could you use these passages to encourage a friend who has doubts and fears?

Praise God for allowing you to see a glimpse of his glory.

A Glorious Glimpse

Now That I Have Your Attention

❖

What do people do to get your attention? A loud horn, whistle, or siren can grab your attention very quickly. The Lord grabbed the disciples' attention in several ways.

**Peter said to Jesus, "Lord, it is good for us to be here.
If you wish, I will put up three shelters—one for you,
one for Moses and one for Elijah."
While he was still speaking, a bright cloud covered them,
and a voice from the cloud said,
"This is my Son, whom I love; with him I am well pleased.
Listen to him!"** MATTHEW 17:4,5

So overwhelmed by the sight of Moses and Elijah, Peter started babbling about making little shelters for the heavenly guests. But God wasn't interested in pitching tents or developing apartments on the mountain. He wanted to grab the disciples' attention one more time by surrounding them with his glory. When he had their full attention, he spoke, "This is my Son, whom I love; with him I am well pleased. Listen to him!" Does God have your attention? God doesn't want your focus to be on what you can build on earth, and he doesn't want you to stay here forever. The Father focuses you on his Son. He was pleased to have his Son be the sinless sacrifice who would win for you a place with him in heaven. There is no other Savior; therefore listen to Jesus who has the words of eternal life!

- At what other times in Jesus' life did the Father use both words and actions to approve of his Son?

- How does seeing God's glory in the Word motivate and encourage you to listen to Jesus?

Thank God for getting your attention so that you focus on Jesus.

A Glorious Glimpse

Don't Be Afraid

❖

Don't be afraid! That is so much easier said than done. Scary masks are meant to frighten people. Scary music can give you the creeps. Scary movies certainly try to make people afraid. Jesus' disciples were very scared. But it wasn't creepy music or a dark setting that was scaring them. What terrified them was God's voice and the brightness of his glory.

**When the disciples heard this, they fell facedown
to the ground, terrified. But Jesus came and touched them.
"Get up," he said. "Don't be afraid."
When they looked up, they saw no one except Jesus.**
MATTHEW 17:6-8

Didn't the disciples want to be with God forever? Then why were the disciples afraid when they saw the Lord's glory? The brightness of God revealed the darkness of their sin. They were not worthy to stand in the Father's presence. The disciples had every reason to fall down in fear because of their sins. But did you notice that Jesus didn't fall down in fear? He is the holy Son of God who pleased his Father in every way. Your God was standing on a mountain 2000 years ago because he came to be your Savior. He lived perfectly for you and died for you. Jesus is near you; don't be afraid.

- Jesus touched his disciples. What does this tell you about Jesus love for you?

- The best part about being in heaven is being with Jesus. What do you think that is going to be like? What will you see? (Read Revelation 21:1-4,22-27.)

Ask the Holy Spirit to fill you with the peace of Jesus' forgiveness so that you aren't afraid.

Selfless

Jesus Gives

❖

Some people are selfless; others are selfish. What is the difference?
Selfish people wonder how they can get something from others. Selfless
people wonder how they can give something to others. Jesus was selfless for
a selfish world.

Now Jesus was going up to Jerusalem. On the way,
he took the Twelve aside and said to them,
"We are going up to Jerusalem, and the Son of Man
will be delivered over to the chief priests and
the teachers of the law. They will condemn him to death
and will hand him over to the Gentiles to be mocked
and flogged and crucified.
On the third day he will be raised to life!" MATTHEW 20:17-19

Jesus was chosen by the Father to be the Lamb of God who
would take away the sin of the world. Your holy God cannot
ignore sin. Sin deserves to be punished, but instead of punishing
you, the Father chose to punish his Son for you. Jesus knew what
was going to happen in Jerusalem, but still he went there. Jesus
went because he loved you. Jesus went to Jerusalem, because there
he would be condemned to die for your sin—he would be the
Savior that you need. Jesus didn't come to earth to selfishly get
as much as he could. Jesus' purpose was to come so that he could
give all that he had—his very life. In your selfless Savior you have
forgiveness and the resurrection from the dead!

- The day on which Jesus died is called Good Friday. How
  can that day be called good?

- Jesus was punished for you. What don't you ever have to
  worry about?

Pray that God gives your heart the peace and joy of salvation.

Selfless

Safe in Jesus

❖

The hail was as big as golf balls as it dropped angrily from the dark sky. The three children in the back seat of the car looked very frightened as the noise grew louder and louder. With tears in her eyes, the little girl asked, "Are we safe?" The family was safe, but the car wasn't. In a matter of minutes, the lights were broken and the metal dented. The car took the beating from the storm but kept the family safe inside. In a similar way, you are safe in Jesus.

**Therefore, there is now no condemnation
for those who are in Christ Jesus,
because through Christ Jesus the law of the Spirit
who gives life has set you free
from the law of sin and death.** ROMANS 8:1,2

Don't be mistaken, there was condemnation—but it wasn't directed toward you. On the cross, Christ Jesus felt God the Father's anger for every sinful act and evil thought. If someone sins, he deserves to die. But God doesn't want sinners to die and be condemned to hell forever. Instead, he condemned his Son on the cross. Jesus is like the car that took the beating from the hail storm and kept the family safe. Jesus took your beating for your sin so that you would be safe. There is now no condemnation for you in Christ Jesus! You have been set free from sin and the power of death. You are now—and will be forever—safe in Christ!

- Christians don't have to fear God's punishment. How does that affect the way they are able to lives their lives?

- How would you respond if someone asked you, "How do I know if Jesus loves me?"

Pray for the Spirit to move you to spread the good news of Jesus.

Selfless

Sour Milk

❖

Have you ever smelled sour milk? Yuck! When milk turns sour, you want to leave the cap on or the stink will fill the house. But do you know what can make your house smell worse than sour milk? It is the sour attitude of selfishness.

**Now Israel loved Joseph more than any of his other sons,
because he had been born to him in his old age;
and he made an ornate robe for him.
When his brothers saw that their father loved him
more than any of them, they hated him and
could not speak a kind word to him.** GENESIS 37:3,4

The sour attitude of selfishness was strong in Joseph's family. His brothers wanted their father's love. They wanted nice gifts too! If you popped the cap off of your heart, would the stink of selfishness fill the room? Are you usually happy when someone else gets something new, or are you jealous? Do you ever say, "It's mine—you can't have one"? Are you ever tempted to think just of yourself and not care about others? Your home probably has been filled with the stink of selfishness. Jesus' home never was. Instead of wanting to be served, Jesus came to serve. He loved you so much that he served you by giving his life as a payment for all of your selfish sins. Jesus didn't scream out, "It's mine!" Instead he died on the cross to say, "I'm yours!" Such love and forgiveness is the sweetest message that your heart could hear.

- Jesus saved you from selfishness by being perfectly selfless. How can you show your thankfulness to Jesus through your attitude?

- What godly attitudes would you like to see in your family?

Pray that Jesus' love creates pleasant attitudes in yourself and your family.

Just What I Wanted

Wanted

❖

It feels good to be wanted. If you're wanted by friends, you feel like you belong to a group. Your family wants you, which makes you feel loved. It would feel terrible to be unwanted. A man in the Bible knew how terrible it felt.

A man was there by the name of Zacchaeus; he was a chief tax collector and was wealthy. He wanted to see who Jesus was, but because he was short he could not see over the crowd. So he ran ahead and climbed a sycamore-fig tree to see him, since Jesus was coming that way. When Jesus reached the spot, he looked up and said to him, "Zacchaeus, come down immediately. I must stay at your house today." LUKE 19:2-5

Zacchaeus was wealthy because he over collected—he got rich by stealing from his own Jewish people. There might have been a second reason, in addition to being short, that kept him from seeing Jesus—it's possible no one would let this unwanted man through the crowd. It is understandable that Zacchaeus wanted to see the One who could do miracles and preach with authority. What is remarkable is that Jesus wanted to see him! Jesus wanted to spend time with a man no one wanted. There may be times when you feel lonely or even unwanted. But you are never unwanted. Jesus wants to hear from you and spend time with you. He desires to be with you.

- Jesus knew Zacchaeus' name and his sin, yet he wanted to stay with him. How should we treat others even if they made a bad mistake and sinned?

- In what ways can Jesus "stay at your house today"?

Ask God to use you to share Jesus' love with someone who feels unwanted.

Just What I Wanted

Wanted Change

❖

Some people like to follow the same old routine, while others like to mix it up and prefer not to have a schedule at all. Some absolutely hate change, but others love it. Do you like change? God does and he actually causes it.

**All the people saw this and began to mutter,
"He has gone to be the guest of a sinner."
But Zacchaeus stood up and said to the Lord,
"Look, Lord! Here and now I give half of my possessions
to the poor, and if I have cheated anybody out of anything,
I will pay back four times the amount."** LUKE 19:7,8

The crowd didn't think that Jesus should talk with Zacchaeus or spend time with him. They thought that Zacchaeus was a worse sinner than they were and that he could never change. But the message that he heard about Jesus did change him! The Spirit of God created faith in his heart; through faith, he called Jesus Lord. Immediately he started to change: He promised that he would support the poor and right past wrongs by paying back the people he had cheated out of money. Jesus is the Savior who frees you from sin. He doesn't free you so that you continue to sin. No longer do you live like the rest of the world, but you live for Jesus because his love, forgiveness, and power have changed you.

- What are some ways you can show that you are different from the rest of the world?

- You aren't less sinful than anyone else. Instead of thinking you are better than others, how can you show that Jesus has changed your heart?

Pray that the Holy Spirit fills you with a strong desire to follow Christ.

Just What I Wanted

You're the Person I Am Looking For

❖

Jesus is the King of Glory whom the angels praise. He is the eternal God who possesses all power, authority, and honor in heaven and on earth! What could the majestic Lord ever want?

Jesus said to [Zacchaeus], "Today salvation has come to this house, because this man, too, is a son of Abraham. For the Son of Man came to seek and to save the lost."
LUKE 19:9,10

Zacchaeus was the sinner most people despised. He was a cheat and a thief who loved wealth. But on the day Jesus visited him, Zacchaeus experienced a love that was greater than his love for money. Zacchaeus was a sinner who was completely lost and deserved hell. Jesus did not ignore him as if he didn't exist nor did he avoid him like he had some weird disease. The King of Glory sought him out! Why? The same reason that Jesus sought your heart—without Jesus you would be lost. Jesus' purpose was to save those who can't save themselves. Jesus rejoices when the sinners, whom the world considers to be the worst, repent and experience his forgiveness. Your guilt is gone. Your sin has been forgiven, and salvation is yours because you were the person Jesus came to seek and to save.

- Jesus didn't speak these Bible passages to the crowd but to Zacchaeus. What does this tell you about your Savior?

- How did Jesus seek and save your soul?

- How can you be involved with seeking and saving souls in a world of lost sinners?

Ask the Lord to equip you and all believers to proclaim the good news of forgiveness so the lost may be found.

The Sacrifice Delivered

Just as God Promised

❖

It was Sunday of Holy Week, and Jesus was right outside the sacred city of Jerusalem. The disciples had come to expect that Jesus could do the spectacular, and once again he did.

As they approached Jerusalem and came to Bethphage on the Mount of Olives, Jesus sent two disciples, saying to them, "Go to the village ahead of you, and at once you will find a donkey tied there, with her colt by her. Untie them and bring them to me. If anyone says anything to you, tell him that the Lord needs them, and he will send them right away." This took place to fulfill what was spoken through the prophet:

**"Say to the Daughter of Zion,
'See, your king comes to you,
gentle and riding on a donkey,
on a colt, the foal of a donkey.'"** MATTHEW 21:1-5

What spectacular thing did Jesus do? He showed that he was all knowing; he knew the donkeys were tied up ahead of them before they even got there! He knew exactly what was going to happen—that is spectacular. But why it was happening is even more incredible. Jesus was fulfilling the 500-year-old prophecy of Zechariah. God had promised that the King would come riding on a donkey. Jesus was going to make it very clear that the King of salvation had arrived, just as God had promised.

- The donkey was considered a humble animal. Why then was the donkey the perfect animal for Jesus to ride into Jerusalem?

- Why is it important for you to know both the Old and New Testament Scriptures?

Praise Jesus as the King who fulfills all of his promises.

The Sacrifice Delivered

Extremely Special

❖

What is the Sunday before Easter called? On Palm Sunday we remember the day Jesus rode into Jerusalem on a donkey. Why is Palm Sunday considered such a special event?

**"Go to the village ahead of you, and as you enter it,
you will find a colt tied there,
which no one has ever ridden.
Untie it and bring it here."
They brought it to Jesus,
threw their cloaks on the colt
and put Jesus on it.** LUKE 19:30,35

The colt that Jesus sat upon never had been ridden or used for work. An animal that never had a burden placed on it was used for religious purposes; carrying the Savior was the most sacred task this donkey would ever perform. Remember that this was Passover Week. According to Exodus 12:3, on this day the Jews would have selected for themselves the lamb they would sacrifice and eat for the Passover meal later in the week. Who was Jesus? He came to earth to be the Lamb of God who would take away the sin of the world! He was the Lamb who was being carried into Jerusalem on Palm Sunday to be sacrificed on the cross on Friday. The colt had a special purpose. Palm Sunday, the day on which the sacrificial lambs were selected for Passover, was indeed very special. But we do more than think of the significance of this day; we cherish the Savior who directed the disciples to get the colt. We cherish Jesus who willingly sat upon the colt in order to be delivered into Jerusalem as your sacrifice. Such love—such a Savior—is extremely special indeed!

- If someone asked why you celebrate Palm Sunday, how would you respond?

Thank Jesus for his gracious willingness to be your sacrifice.

The Sacrifice Delivered

Caught Up in The Crowd

❖

Have you ever gotten caught up in excitement with a crowd? Maybe you were at a big game with your friends. When the game got really exciting, perhaps your friends started yelling for your team, and you couldn't help but yell too? It can be easy to get caught up in the crowd.

**The crowds that went ahead of him and
those that followed shouted,
"Hosanna to the Son of David!"
"Blessed is he who comes in the name of the Lord!"
"Hosanna in the highest heaven!"
When Jesus entered Jerusalem, the whole city was stirred
and asked, "Who is this?"
The crowds answered, "This is Jesus,
the prophet from Nazareth in Galilee."** MATTHEW 21:9-11

The large crowd was excited as they shouted words of praise. *Hosanna* means "to help or save." Yet some had to ask, "Who is this?" The answer they received shows that the crowd wasn't fully aware of who Jesus was. They called him "the prophet from Nazareth in Galilee." It can be easy for us to get caught up in the crowd, even a religious crowd. God doesn't want you to only shout words of thanks and praise with your mouth, but also with your heart. Jesus *is* the great Prophet who proclaimed the Word of God, but he is more than a prophet: He is God's Son and your Savior. You follow him, not because the crowd does, but because Jesus is the Lord who saves you.

- How might it be possible to get caught up with the crowd in a worship service but still not worship with your heart?

- Jesus went to the cross for people who didn't even know him to be the Son of God. Why is that comforting to you?

Ask the Spirit to focus your heart on Jesus as the Savior even when the crowd doesn't.

In the Hour of Trial

Jesus Prayed

❖

What do you do when you are frightened or overwhelmed with sadness?
Jesus doesn't only teach you what to do, but he does it perfectly for you!

**Then Jesus went with his disciples to a place
called Gethsemane, and he said to them,
"Sit here while I go over there and pray."
Then he said to them, "My soul is overwhelmed with sorrow
to the point of death. Stay here and keep watch with me."
Going a little farther, he fell with his face
to the ground and prayed.** MATTHEW 26:36,38,39

Your Savior was so overwhelmed with sorrow and was so upset that he felt like he could die. But Jesus didn't complain or gripe about what he had to do. Jesus didn't sinfully worry whether God was going to help him, or whether God could help him. Jesus prayed. Jesus went to his Father for strength, trusting that his Father would answer him and do what was best. The Father did what was best—for you! God gave you a Savior who perfectly trusted so that you can have Jesus' perfection through faith. God gave you a Savior who always did his Father's will, so that you wouldn't be overwhelmed with death but overjoyed with forgiveness, life, and the certain hope of salvation. Jesus prayed perfectly for you!

- What does it mean for you to keep watch?

- How can it be helpful to gather with others who pray for you and with you?

- Jesus felt the deep emotions of being overwhelmed with sorrow. What encouragement does that give you when you go to him in prayer?

Pray that the Spirit gives you a heart that is quick to pray and slow to worry.

In the Hour of Trial

Willing and Weak

❖

The championship game was about to start. The opposing team was ready and prepared to do battle. The closest friends of the star player had front row tickets—and they were asleep! What?

Then he returned to his disciples and found them sleeping. "Couldn't you men keep watch with me for one hour?" he asked Peter. "Watch and pray so that you will not fall into temptation. The spirit is willing, but the flesh is weak." MATTHEW 26:40,41

Jesus may have been the star player, but the disciples were involved in the battle too. Weren't the disciples willing to fight for Jesus? Yes, and they sincerely promised that they would die with him. Peter would later pull out a sword and cut off an enemy's ear for Jesus. The disciples' hearts were willing, but their bodies were weak. Your body is weak too. No, you might have huge muscles, but your body has limitations. Your heart loves Jesus, but then your eyes become sleepy during church. You want to read Jesus' Word more, but your mind starts thinking about other things and forgets. Not for one hour—not for one moment—have you had enough strength to fight off all temptations. But Jesus did. Even in his weakest moments when Jesus felt the toughest temptations, he never sinned. Jesus did watch, pray, and conquer temptation for you!

- Satan likes to attack when you are at your weakest. When are your weak moments? Why is it important to understand your weak moments when you are fighting temptation?

- Why is it foolish to rely on your body and your mind? Why is it wise to rely on Jesus and his Word?

Ask Jesus to keep you strong through his Word and faithful in prayer.

In the Hour of Trial

Your Will, Not Mine

❖

When you play a game, whose rules do you like to follow? You could be one of those rare people who likes to follow the rules of others, or you might be like most people who want to use their own rules. Even when life was difficult, Jesus continued to follow his Father's desires and teaches us to do the same.

> **He went away a second time and prayed,**
> **"My Father, if it is not possible for this cup**
> **to be taken away unless I drink it,**
> **may your will be done."** MATTHEW 26:42

The Father sent his Son to earth to rescue sinners by being punished on the cross for them. How terrible it was for Jesus to know the suffering that was in his near future! However, he wasn't about to run away or even change the rules of life's game. Jesus wasn't willing to change his Father's holy will for him, but he was willing to follow it. Life isn't always pleasant, nor will you always understand the suffering you go through. But you can understand and trust in the suffering Jesus went through for you. His suffering means that you are forgiven for all the times you wanted to change God's will and Word because it just seemed easier and more pleasant. Jesus' suffering means you are forgiven and need not fear being punished by God. Jesus empowers you as his dear child to pray, "May your will be done!"

- How do you know what God's will is for you? If you want a strong prayer life, what do you also need?

- You don't change God's Word, but God's Word changes you. Why is this comforting?

Pray that God's will is done through you.

The King Before the Governor

The King

❖

What pictures come to mind when you think of a king? Is the picture in your mind of a thin or heavyset man? Do you perhaps picture an animated character from a movie? We probably all have a picture in our mind of what we would expect a king to look like. The crowd that brought Jesus to the Roman governor had their own idea of what a king should be—and Jesus wasn't it.

Pilate then went back inside the palace, summoned Jesus and asked him, "Are you the king of the Jews?"

Jesus said, "My kingdom is not of this world. If it were, my servants would fight to prevent my arrest by the Jewish leaders. But now my kingdom is from another place."

"You are a king, then!" said Pilate.

Jesus answered, "You say that I am a king. In fact, the reason I was born and came into the world is to testify to the truth. Everyone on the side of truth listens to me." JOHN 18:33,36,37

Jesus didn't look like a king. Jesus didn't have any subjects fighting for him the way a king would. He had no earthly wealth, throne, or castle. Could Jesus really be a king? Yes! But Jesus' kingdom is not of this world. Jesus doesn't rule his kingdom with swords, tanks, or bombs. Jesus rules with his truth! Jesus conquered your heart with his Word and rules in your heart as the King who won for you full forgiveness. Is Jesus a king? Yes, he is your loving King both now and forever!

- Why didn't the crowd or Pilate recognize Jesus as their King?

- What do believers who belong to Jesus' kingdom long to do? What does it mean to listen to Jesus?

Ask Jesus to rule your heart by keeping you connected to the gospel.

The King Before the Governor

Rejection Hurts

❖

How would you feel if your family decided to take someone else to Disney World instead of you? It would hurt your feelings and probably cause you to ask, "Why?" You love your family! Why would they choose someone else over you? Jesus endured terrible sorrow and heartbreaking rejection for you.

"It is your custom for me to release to you one prisoner at the time of the Passover. Do you want me to release 'the king of the Jews'?"
They shouted back, "No, not him! Give us Barabbas!"
Now Barabbas had taken part in an uprising. JOHN 18:39,40

Jesus loved the crowd, but the crowd didn't love Jesus. You haven't ever shouted for Barabbas to be released, but have you ever wanted something more than Jesus? Was sleep on Sunday morning more important than worshiping your King? Have you ever invited violent images into your mind through video games or movies as if violence and revenge are good things, even though Jesus says they aren't? Jesus felt the hurt of rejection. Jesus was willing to be humiliated so that you would never be rejected by his Father in heaven. Jesus felt the punishment of being unloved in your place so that through his suffering God would be pleased with you. How pleased is God with you? He calls you his child whom he will never reject.

- Talk about how setting priorities in your life shows love and thankfulness for Jesus.

- Jesus was rejected by God so that you never will be. Why is this truth so powerful when you feel guilty for your sin?

Thank Jesus for his willingness to feel the hurt of rejection so that you can be with your heavenly Father forever.

The King Before the Governor

Not a Time to Feel Sorry

❖

When someone scrapes a knee or breaks an arm, it is easy to feel sorry for him or her. But when you are reading about Jesus' suffering, don't feel sorry for him. Instead, marvel at his love and his willingness to suffer for you.

Then the governor's soldiers took Jesus into the Praetorium and gathered the whole company of soldiers around him. They stripped him and put a scarlet robe on him, and then twisted together a crown of thorns and set it on his head. They put a staff in his right hand. Then they knelt in front of him and mocked him. "Hail, king of the Jews!" they said. They spit on him, and took the staff and struck him on the head again and again. After they had mocked him, they took off the robe and put his own clothes on him. Then they led him away to crucify him. MATTHEW 27:27-31

Ambulances turn on their sirens and drive as fast as they can to help people. Reading about how Jesus was beaten and mistreated may make you want to run to help him. But Jesus didn't need to be rescued. He was suffering in order to rescue you from the punishment your sin deserves! Don't feel sorry for Jesus because of the way he suffered; trust that his suffering means that God isn't angry with you. Trust that the blood that Jesus shed paid for your sin, which means that you belong to Jesus who will always be your heavenly King.

- Jesus wasn't powerless. What kept him from fighting back or using his almighty power?

- Do you ever have to worry if God is going to punish you for sin?

Pray that the joy of salvation fills your heart with peace.

Jesus Died for Me

A Time of Mourning

❖

How do people show their sadness and grief? Black is a common color often worn to funerals in the United States as a symbol of sadness. However, some cultures teach that the colors gray, blue, purple, and even yellow are symbols of sorrow and mourning. There are many ways that people show sorrow, but how does nature show that it is sad?

From noon until three in the afternoon darkness came over all the land. About three in the afternoon Jesus cried out in a loud voice, "Eli, Eli, lema sabachthani?" (which means "My God, my God, why have you forsaken me?"). MATTHEW 27:45,46

Even creation mourned for three hours over the agony of its Creator who was nailed to the cross. God wrapped the sky in darkness to show that Jesus' death was no ordinary death. God's Son suffered every sin that you have done and experienced the torment of hell for all your guilt. God the Father left Jesus and showed him no love! Why would God do that to his Son with whom he was pleased? Why would God forsake his Son as a sinner? "Why have you forsaken me?" Jesus asked. You know the answer to that question. The Father forsook his Son because of his great love for you! The Father punished Jesus so that you would never have to be punished or face the fires of hell. Oh, the depth of Jesus' suffering! Oh, the depth of his love for you!

- Darkness came over the land from noon until 3 P.M. How do you know that had to be a miracle from God?

- Imagine that a friend says, "I have done some bad things in my life. I'm afraid that God is really going to punish me." How would you respond?

Praise God for being merciful to you.

Jesus Died for Me

It's Not Fair!

❖

How would you feel if you and your friend did the exact same thing, and you got into trouble, but your friend didn't? You would probably feel better if he or she got caught and got into trouble too. That would only be fair, right? Jesus doesn't treat you fairly, and you can be thankful for that.

**The other criminal rebuked him. "Don't you fear God,"
he said, "since you are under the same sentence?
We are punished justly, for we are getting what our deeds
deserve. But this man has done nothing wrong."
Then he said, "Jesus, remember me
when you come into your kingdom."
Jesus answered him, "Truly I tell you,
today you will be with me in paradise."** LUKE 23:40-43

The criminal couldn't say, "It's not fair!" He admitted that he deserved to be crucified because of his crimes. It was fair that he was being punished for what he had done. It would be fair for God to punish all sinners by sending them to hell! What was unfair is that Jesus was being punished even though he had no sin and committed no crime. But the name Jesus means "he saves." Jesus was on the cross paying for every sin and crime that the criminal had committed. Jesus paid for every sin you ever did and every evil thought that ever entered your mind. Your Savior died for you so that he could promise that you will be with him in paradise. Totally unfair!

- When do believers go to heaven? (Look at Jesus' response to the criminal's request.)

- What does Jesus' response tell us about the criminal's faith?

Pray that Jesus keeps you in the faith through his Word so that you will spend eternity with him.

Jesus Died for Me

It Is Finished!

❖

When you give money to a cashier to buy something in a store, what does the cashier hand back to you? You get your change back along with your receipt. The receipt shows that you have paid for the item and you are free to walk out of the store with your new treasure; it belongs to you.

When he had received the drink, Jesus said, "It is finished." With that, he bowed his head and gave up his spirit.
JOHN 19:30

"It is finished" is one of the most powerful truths in the Bible. It means that Jesus completed everything necessary to save you. Does God expect more from you before you are saved? No! Do you have to live the best life you can so that you can go to heaven? No! Jesus tells you that nothing more needs to be done for your salvation. Christ didn't redeem you with gold or silver. He didn't use a credit card so that you could pay him back later. He willingly shed his blood on the cross and gave up his life for you. Your body and soul are bought and paid for. It is finished! You are saved and belong to Jesus.

- Jesus paid the price that saves you. There is nothing more that you could give; nothing more you could do for your salvation. Why then do you live your life for Jesus?

- How would you answer someone who says, "I wonder if I have done enough good things to get into heaven?"

Thank God for the full and free salvation that is yours through faith in Jesus.

He Is Risen

Now I Have Told You

❖

It feels good to be able to tell someone good news! It can be terrible to have to tell someone bad news. The women who followed Jesus had been sharing what they thought was the most terrible news ever—Jesus was dead! They weren't expecting any good news when they went to Jesus' grave early on Easter morning.

**After the Sabbath, at dawn on the first day of the week,
Mary Magdalene and the other Mary went to look at the tomb.
The angel said to the women, "Do not be afraid,
for I know that you are looking for Jesus, who was crucified.
He is not here; he has risen, just as he said.
Come and see the place where he lay.
Then go quickly and tell his disciples:
'He has risen from the dead and is going ahead
of you into Galilee. There you will see him.'
Now I have told you."** MATTHEW 28:1,5-7

The women didn't need to be afraid, and the angels didn't have to keep the good news to themselves any longer. Jesus was alive! Jesus conquered death. This means that you don't have to be afraid, not even of dying. Because Jesus lives, you too will rise from the grave and live with Jesus forever. Like the women, you too have a wonderful mission. Tell others that Jesus has risen from the dead and that they too will see the living Lord. Alleluia! He is risen. He is risen indeed. Alleluia!

- What does Jesus' resurrection teach us about our Savior that can comfort and cheer us every day?

- Jesus doesn't send angels into the world to spread the gospel. He chose to send you. Why can you be confident as you share the good news?

Praise the Lord for giving you the victory over death.

He Is Risen

He Is the One

❖

How do you recognize police officers? They generally wear uniforms and carry badges. Police officers want you to know who they are because they are there to help you. How do you know who the true Savior is? What makes you sure that Jesus is the one who will help and save you?

Paul, a servant of Christ Jesus, called to be an apostle and set apart for the gospel of God—the gospel he promised beforehand through his prophets in the Holy Scriptures regarding his Son, who as to his earthly life was a descendant of David, and who through the Spirit of holiness was appointed the Son of God in power by his resurrection from the dead: Jesus Christ our Lord. ROMANS 1:1-4

The Holy Spirit didn't pin a badge to Jesus. Instead, he raised Jesus from the dead so you can be absolutely confident that he is God's Son. Jesus is true God who was born as true man to live a perfect life for you. Jesus is the One who was chosen by God to be the sacrifice that would wash you clean and free you from all sin. Jesus is your living Lord who rules your heart with the promise that he defeated death so that you can live with him forever. You know Jesus to be true God, but not by a common badge or uniform. You know Jesus to be God's Son by his resurrection from the dead!

- There is only one Son of God, and you know him! What are you going to do with such awesome knowledge?

Pray that the Spirit strengthens you through the good news of the resurrection from the dead so that you can boldly share that news with others.

He Is Risen

The Victory Is Hidden No More

❖

Do you think that Jesus' enemies were happy or sad when he was crucified? They were the ones who shouted for Jesus to be nailed to the cross. Jesus' enemies thought the Friday on which Jesus died was good because they wanted him dead. They thought they had finally won when Jesus was placed in the tomb. The Bible teaches that even though Jesus was dead in the tomb, the victory already belonged to him and to you.

He was delivered over to death for our sins and was raised to life for our justification. ROMANS 4:25

Jesus was punished for you on the cross so that you would not be punished by God. Your sin was paid through Jesus' death. But who knew that Jesus saved the world on the cross? The disciples weren't celebrating behind the locked door. The enemies were celebrating that they were finally rid of Jesus. The truth that your sin was paid for was hidden from the world. Jesus didn't want this beautiful truth hidden, so on the third day he rose to life to openly show the world that you were justified. Jesus declared you to be innocent and free from all guilt. Jesus won the victory on the cross and showed that the victory is yours by rising from the dead.

- Do you ever feel guilty for the things that you do? How does Jesus' resurrection from the dead bring relief and comfort to your heart?

- You are innocent in Jesus right now! When God looks at you, he sees the perfection of Jesus. What does such a bold promise encourage you to do?

Pray that the Spirit fills you with the joy of salvation through the message of Jesus.

WEEK 48 DAY 1

Everlasting Life

Safe With Jesus

❖

Does death frighten you? Death is unpleasant because it takes from you the people you love and depend on. When you die you are taken away from what you know, your family, and the things that bring you joy. It is true; you can't take your stuff with you when you die. But it is also true that death can't take you away from Jesus.

My sheep listen to my voice; I know them, and they follow me. I give them eternal life, and they shall never perish; no one will snatch them out of my hand. JOHN 10:27,28

Through faith in Jesus, you are his sheep whom he knows and who follow him. Jesus loves his sheep so much that he gives them the gift of eternal life! You do not have to worry about going to hell. You don't have to wonder if you will suffer or what will happen after this life. Jesus promises that you will be with him forever because no one can pull, pry, or steal you from your Savior. The precious hands that hold onto you are the precious hands that received nails for you. Can your sin take you away from Jesus? No, he forgives you. Can death pull you from Jesus? No, he conquered death and on the third day he rose. Can the devil snatch you away? No! Jesus defeated the devil, and Satan has no hold on you. Jesus holds you. Jesus saved you. Jesus gives you eternal life, and you will be safe with him forever!

- Who listens to Jesus' voice?

- What promises does Jesus give to you that comfort you even in the face of death?

- Who will you be with forever?

Thank Jesus for the good news of eternal life.

Everlasting Life

The Resurrection and the Life

❖

Jesus didn't run to help sick Lazarus. Jesus waited two days before he set out for Lazarus' house. Jesus waited until his friend was dead. Didn't Jesus care? He cared so much that he wanted you to hear and see his power.

Jesus said to her, "I am the resurrection and the life. The one who believes in me will live, even though he dies; and whoever lives and believes in me will never die. Do you believe this?"

Then Jesus said, "Did I not tell you that if you believe, you will see the glory of God?"

When he had said this, Jesus called in a loud voice, "Lazarus, come out!" The dead man came out, his hands and feet wrapped with strips of linen, and a cloth around his face. JOHN 11:25,26,40,43,44

Why did Jesus allow Lazarus to die? He wanted to show you his glory. "Lazarus, come out!" Why does Jesus allow those he loves to die? Jesus doesn't only want you to see his glory one day, but he wants you to experience it. If you die, Jesus will call you from your grave so both your soul and body will live. Those who believe and die will live! Those who live and believe in Jesus will never die. Do you believe this? Yes, Lord, we believe that you are the resurrection and the life.

- Why is it sad when someone dies? Why can Christians have joy even at funerals?

- What did Jesus use to raise Lazarus from the dead? What is going to comfort your heart in times of sadness?

Ask Jesus to comfort with his promises the hearts of those who have lost a loved one.

Everlasting Life

Just Visiting

❖

Where would you like to vacation? It can be fun to take trips to the mountains, the beach, or new places you have never seen before. It is good to get away, but it is also good to be home. God's Word teaches that you are just visiting here on earth for a little while, because heaven is your home.

**Our citizenship is in heaven.
And we eagerly await a Savior from there,
the Lord Jesus Christ, who, by the power
that enables him to bring everything under his control,
will transform our lowly bodies so that
they will be like his glorious body.** PHILIPPIANS 3:20,21

When you visit a new place, especially if it is in another country, it can sometimes be awkward. The language may be different. The food can be unique. You might even look different from those who live there. Right away people would be able to tell that you don't belong there.

Your citizenship is in heaven. God is promising that heaven is your home. You won't stick out there. You won't feel like you're just visiting or you don't belong. Heaven is your home because Jesus is your Savior. Your sins have been forgiven, and Jesus is coming himself to take you home to be with him forever. Not only will it be a glorious experience, but you will be glorified. Your body will not have any bruises, scrapes, pains, or sickness. You will have a glorified body like Jesus. You will be filled with joy and life! Truly there is no place like home.

- Heaven is your home. How should you feel about this earth and the stuff you have?

- What comfort and hope does this passage give you?

Ask God to keep your heart focused on the treasures you have in heaven.

Doubt No More!

Eyes in Your Heart

❖

You can't believe everything! Parents tell you not to believe everything you see on your computer screen, because it may not be true. You doubt your friend who tells you a story that seems to be ridiculous. You don't want to look foolish for believing something that was made-up. Thomas wasn't able to believe something that seemed impossible to him.

Now Thomas (also known as Didymus), one of the Twelve, was not with the disciples when Jesus came. So the other disciples told him, "We have seen the Lord!"

But he said to them, "Unless I see the nail marks in his hands and put my finger where the nails were, and put my hand into his side, I will not believe." JOHN 20:24,25

Thomas didn't only want proof that he could see, but proof he could feel. Has doubt and unbelief been tempting you? The sinful nature in everyone relies on the eyes in the head and ignores the eyes of faith. How do you think Thomas felt when he wouldn't believe and thought Jesus was dead? When you refuse to believe God's promises, you lose out on God's blessings of hope and peace. Why can you believe that Jesus is alive? He is the Lord who conquered death! Jesus, your Savior, has the nail holes in his hands to prove that he died for your unbelief and forgives you all of your doubts. You have eyes of faith that have seen the Lord!

- Through faith we receive God's blessings. What blessings do you sometimes forfeit because of sinful doubt?

- Jesus rose from the dead! How does his resurrection give you confidence in his promises?

Pray for a heart that believes even when your eyes can't see.

Doubt No More!

Be at Peace!

❖

Have you ever been so sure that you were right only to find out you actually were wrong? Maybe you even argue with your parents because you think you know better than they do. Have you ever gotten into a fight with a friend or your sibling because you just had to be right? How did you feel when someone proves you wrong? Try to imagine how Thomas felt.

A week later his disciples were in the house again, and Thomas was with them. Though the doors were locked, Jesus came and stood among them and said, "Peace be with you!" Then he said to Thomas, "Put your finger here; see my hands. Reach out your hand and put it into my side. Stop doubting and believe." JOHN 20:26,27

The shame must have been overwhelming! Would you have let out a little scream? Would you have run away and hid? Would you have cried? Jesus appeared to Thomas because he loved him. What was the first thing Jesus said to him? "Peace be with you!" Jesus wasn't there to punish Thomas. Jesus was there because he was already punished on the cross for Thomas' sins of unbelief and doubt. Jesus was punished for the times you are slow to believe in his promises too. But he appears to us on the pages of Scripture and says, "Be at peace!" He forgave Thomas, and he forgives you.

- How do you think Thomas felt when he finally believed that his Savior had risen?

- Jesus tells us to stop doubting and believe. What can we do—what do we need to do—when we find ourselves worried and afraid?

- What does it mean that you are at peace with God?

Praise Jesus for the peace that only he can give.

Doubt No More!

Blessed Are You!

❖

Thomas' heart must have been pounding in his chest. He had made the bold statement that he would not believe unless he stuck his finger into Jesus' hands. His heart was stubborn with unbelief until Jesus appeared and invited him to touch the nail holes.

Thomas said to him, "My Lord and my God!"

Then Jesus told him, "Because you have seen me, you have believed; blessed are those who have not seen and yet have believed." JOHN 20:28,29

Before this, Thomas thought Jesus was dead. Thomas wouldn't believe—that is, until he saw Jesus standing before him. He confessed, "My Lord and my God!" You confess the same thing but have never seen Jesus. You have never stuck your finger in his hand or side. Yet you believe because you have been blessed by the Holy Spirit with the gift of faith. When you read the words from John 20, the Holy Spirit was working in your heart, strengthening the faith he gave you. The Word is the Spirit's tool that always is powerful and active. You have the power of God! Blessed are you who can confess that Jesus is your Lord and Savior!

- What truths about God do you confess in a worship service? How can you as a family confess Jesus in your home?

- The Word of God is vital for faith. Without the Word, people's faith will shrink and eventually die. What promises does God's Word give that you can use when you have doubts and worries?

Thank the Holy Spirit for the gift of faith.

The Ascended Lord

On a Mission

❖

Jesus had died. Jesus had risen from the dead. The resurrected Savior had spent 40 days teaching his disciples from God's Word. It was time for Jesus to leave and go to heaven. But when the Lord ascended into heaven, he left much behind.

Then they gathered around him and asked him, "Lord, are you at this time going to restore the kingdom to Israel?" He said to them: "It is not for you to know the times or dates the Father has set by his own authority. But you will receive power when the Holy Spirit comes on you; and you will be my witnesses in Jerusalem, and in all Judea and Samaria, and to the ends of the earth." ACTS 1:6-8

Jesus' kingdom isn't about castles, riches, and military power. His kingdom is about forgiveness and grace. Yes, Jesus will return to judge the world, but no one except God knows the time or date. Don't concern yourself with wondering about when Jesus will return. Concern yourself with the mission that Jesus gave you to do. Jesus promised to empower his disciples with the Holy Spirit so that they would be his witnesses. You too have been given the gift of the Holy Spirit through your baptism. The Spirit lives in you and strengthens your faith through his powerful Word. Jesus leaves his believers on earth—he leaves you on earth to witness about him.

- A witness simply tells what he or she has seen and heard. What are some incredible events from Jesus' life that the disciples could tell others?

- What are some of your favorite lessons about Jesus that you like to share with others?

Pray that the Holy Spirit gives his people the power to witness.

The Ascended Lord

No Standing Around

❖

Have you ever released a helium balloon outside? It is neat to watch as the balloon disappears into the sky. Imagine what it must have looked like when Jesus rose high into the sky before his disciples.

**After he said this, he was taken up before their very eyes, and a cloud hid him from their sight. They were looking intently up into the sky as he was going, when suddenly two men dressed in white stood beside them.
"Men of Galilee," they said, "why do you stand here looking into the sky? This same Jesus, who has been taken from you into heaven, will come back in the same way you have seen him go into heaven."** ACTS 1:9-11

Do you think that the disciples' jaws were hanging open? Jesus wasn't filled with helium; Jesus was filled with almighty power and glory! Jesus showed his disciples that he no longer was going to be seen teaching on earth, but that he was going to rule from heaven. The disciples were so amazed at this that they just stared up into the sky. Did they even notice the angels standing there beside them? It was true that Jesus wasn't going to be preaching and teaching visibly, but Jesus would continue proclaiming the good news of forgiveness through his disciples. Jesus still proclaims his good news through you. Don't stand around. There is work to do before Jesus comes back.

- Jesus will come back the same way that he went into heaven. Describe what you will see when Jesus returns.

- Why don't you have to be scared when Jesus returns?

Pray for Jesus to come back quickly so that you can be where he is.

The Ascended Lord

Ruler of All

❖

The champion boxer is the one with the title belt. The champion team proudly wears the T-shirt that declares them to be the best in the world. The champion of the game King of the Hill is the one who is standing on top. How can you be sure that Jesus is the champion?

God placed all things under his feet and appointed him to be head over everything for the church, which is his body, the fullness of him who fills everything in every way. EPHESIANS 1:22,23

There is no title belt around Jesus' waist. He doesn't wear a winner's T-shirt with heaven's logo on it. Yet he is on top. God the Father placed his Son in the position of all authority above everything and everyone in the entire universe! There is no one stronger, wiser, more powerful, more gracious, or more perfect than Christ. No one! What do champions do with their power and glory? Some will sign contracts to do commercials in order to make more money. Some champions will brag and boast. What will your champion do with his power? He will use it for the good of his church. The Lord who conquered death rules for you. Jesus controls the weather, the rulers of the world, and all history with you in mind. Jesus rules so that one day you will rule with him!

- Jesus promises that he will always be in control even when the world seems out of control. What comfort does that bring to your life now?

- If Christ rules all things for the good of his church, what comfort can you have when things go badly in life?

Praise Jesus for ruling for you.

The Holy Spirit's Holiday

The Gift Has Arrived!

❖

Have relatives ever told you to watch for something that will be coming in the mail? How did you know when the package had arrived? The gift Jesus promised his disciples had arrived. They didn't have to be told that it had come, and they didn't have to unwrap it.

When the day of Pentecost came, they were all together in one place. Suddenly a sound like the blowing of a violent wind came from heaven and filled the whole house where they were sitting. They saw what seemed to be tongues of fire that separated and came to rest on each of them. ACTS 2:1-3

The disciples heard what sounded like a violent wind, but they didn't feel the wind. How would you feel if you looked at your family members and saw flames hovering above them? God was telling the disciples that the gift had arrived! The Holy Spirit had come! These miracles were amazing, but the disciples would experience even greater miracles, just as you do. You might not see tongues of fire, but you have seen how the Spirit works in the heart of others as they worship Jesus and sing his praise. You experience the Spirit's power as you grow in your understanding of God's Word and live your life for Jesus. It is not through the sound of wind, but it is through the sound of the gospel that you know the Spirit has come to you.

- Why do you think God used the sound of a violent wind to announce the coming of the Holy Spirit?

- What was God emphasizing by having the tongues of fire rest on each of the disciples?

- How does God let you know that he is personally with you?

Thank the Father and Son for sending you the Holy Spirit.

The Holy Spirit's Holiday

The Delivery Man

❖

By some estimates, 20 million packages are delivered each day in the United States. Jesus has chosen to deliver gifts to you. He doesn't use trucks, vans, boxes, or envelopes. Jesus sends his gifts of forgiveness and salvation through the always dependable Holy Spirit.

All of them were filled with the Holy Spirit and began to speak in other tongues as the Spirit enabled them. Now there were staying in Jerusalem God-fearing Jews from every nation under heaven. When they heard this sound, a crowd came together in bewilderment, because each one heard their own language being spoken. ACTS 2:4-6

While on vacation, have you ever purchased a souvenir to take back home?

In his wisdom, Jesus sent the Holy Spirit to Jerusalem when thousands of visitors were gathered together from many different countries. The Spirit gave the disciples the gift of speaking in different languages so that everyone there could hear about Jesus and the gift of forgiveness. Those who were staying in Jerusalem at the time of Pentecost were able to take home the greatest souvenir ever. They took Jesus back to their countries and shared him with others. The Holy Spirit delivered Jesus' forgiveness to you through the good news of baptism and his Word. You have Jesus and the Holy Spirit who gives you the power to tell others about your Savior.

- How are Christians today able to take the message of Jesus to others in the United States and throughout the world?

- How are Christians able to share the Word with others who speak different languages?

Pray for Christians who are studying different languages in order to proclaim the Word.

The Holy Spirit's Holiday

The Spirit's Tools

❖

What tool do you need if you were going to plant a tree? You need a shovel to dig the hole. The Holy Spirit gives you the gift of faith. What tool does he use to create and strengthen faith in a person's heart?

Peter replied, "Repent and be baptized, every one of you, in the name of Jesus Christ for the forgiveness of your sins. And you will receive the gift of the Holy Spirit." Those who accepted his message were baptized, and about three thousand were added to their number that day. ACTS 2:38,41

What shall we do? Peter didn't hand the people a to-do list and say, "Here you go. Work hard, and God will love and forgive you." Through Peter's message, the Holy Spirit showed them their sin and then showed them that Jesus was their Savior. They didn't have to earn forgiveness because Jesus already had earned it for them. Jesus has earned salvation for you. Through your baptism you have received the promise that your sins have been completely washed away. Not only has your heart been washed clean, but it has also been filled up with the Spirit. The Holy Spirit lives in you. It is amazing to think that on the day of Pentecost, 3,000 were baptized! But just as amazing was the day that you were baptized for the forgiveness of all your sins and made a child of God.

- The water of your baptism has dried, but the promises always remain. How can your baptism be a comfort to you every day?

- Think of some ways you can daily be reminded of your baptism.

Pray that the Spirit rules your heart and captures the hearts of others through his Word.

The Ripple Effect

A Big Splash

❖

Have you ever thrown a stone into a pond or puddle? A big splash is followed by ripples spreading out from the center. God's people in Jerusalem were being persecuted and even killed. The Lord, however, used even this terrible time in history to do his amazing work of saving others. Like the ripples in a lake, the Word of God spread farther and farther as persecuted Christians spread the message of Christ throughout the world.

Those who had been scattered preached the word wherever they went. Philip went down to a city in Samaria and proclaimed the Messiah there. When the crowds heard Philip and saw the signs he performed, they all paid close attention to what he said. For with shrieks, impure spirits came out of many, and many who were paralyzed or lame were healed. So there was great joy in that city. ACTS 8:4-8

Philip loved his Savior, and when he had to leave Jerusalem, he took the message of Jesus wherever he went. God has blessed most Americans with the gift of travel. We travel for vacation, for work, for school, and for shopping. When you travel, have you been looking for the opportunity to share Jesus? By performing miracles through him, Christ showed Philip that he didn't have to be shy when proclaiming the good news. The same Jesus who drove out demons and healed the lame is the Jesus who gives you the joy of salvation. You have the message of forgiveness that will bring great joy to others. Be a ripple that proclaims what Jesus has done for you!

- Think of the places you go and list some people to whom you can proclaim Jesus.

- Who have been the bold people in your life who proclaimed Jesus to you?

- What are some of the promises that you are eager to share with others?

Pray for boldness to proclaim Christ.

The Ripple Effect

More Than Knowing

❖

Would you be good at playing Bible trivia? It can be fun to see how many Bible facts you know. But knowledge of facts and figures isn't the only thing that God wants you to have.

Then Philip ran up to the chariot and heard the man reading Isaiah the prophet. "Do you understand what you are reading?" Philip asked.

"How can I," he said, "unless someone explains it to me?" So he invited Philip to come up and sit with him. Then Philip began with that very passage of Scripture and told him the good news about Jesus. ACTS 8:30,31,35

The man in the chariot could read the Word but didn't understand what it meant. Most likely you have a Bible in your home and attend church. You can read and listen to the Word. You may even have some Bible passages memorized. But God wants you to know his Word with more than just your brain. The man in the chariot wanted to understand what God was saying so that he could know the truth with his heart. Understanding the Word of God does take hard work as you read, reread, study, and memorize it. It may even take a parent, a friend, a teacher or pastor to explain some of it to you. But as you grow in your understanding, you will grow in your relationship with Jesus. You will grow by the power of the Spirit to know the good news of a Savior from sin with your head and with your heart.

- What is it called when we know the truth of God's Word with our heart?

- What are some things that you can use to grow in your understanding of God's Word?

Pray for those who teach and preach the Word.

155

The Ripple Effect

Thirsty Souls

❖

If you get thwirsty, you take a drink to quench your thirst. But something strange and wonderful happens when thirsty souls take a drink of God's Word. When you are in the Word, the thirst for the good news of Jesus doesn't go away but gets stronger.

As they traveled along the road, they came to some water and the eunuch said, "Look, here is water. What can stand in the way of my being baptized?" And he gave orders to stop the chariot. Then both Philip and the eunuch went down into the water and Philip baptized him. When they came up out of the water, the Spirit of the Lord suddenly took Philip away, and the eunuch did not see him again, but went on his way rejoicing. ACTS 8:36-39

The eunuch understood that Jesus was his Savior from sin. But he just couldn't get enough of the soul-refreshing forgiveness that Jesus had to offer. He wanted to receive God's loving kindness through the waters of Baptism. You know Jesus as your Savior, but that doesn't mean you should ever stop being in the Word. God's truth is what keeps your faith alive and keeps you connected to Jesus. God's Word quenches your guilty conscience by giving you forgiveness and filling your heart with peace. The more you are in God's Word, the more you will desire to be with your Jesus and receive his blessings. Your spiritual thirst is both quenched and increased through the Word.

- Desiring God's Word is a wonderful spiritual thirst to have. Why do you desire to be in God's Word?

- The eunuch went away rejoicing. What is it about God's Word that makes you excited and joyful?

Ask the Holy Spirit to increase your desire to listen to God.